WORKING PARENTS CAN RAISE SMART KIDS

The "Time-Starved" Parent's Guide to Helping Your Child Succeed in School

John E. Beaulieu, Ph.D.
Alex Granzin, Ph.D.
with Deborah S. Romaine

PARKLAND PRESS, Inc. Tacoma, Washington

Copyright ©1999 John E. Beaulieu, Ph.D. & Alex Granzin, Ph.D.
All rights reserved.

No portion of this book may be reproduced or used in any form, or by any means, except for the inclusion of brief quotations in a review, without prior written permission of the publisher.

Cover design, publication design and layout by Roxanne Carrington
Cover images copyright ©1997 PhotoDisc, Inc.
Illustrations by Roxanne Carrington

10 9 8 7 6 5 4 3 2 1

Printed in the United States of America

Library of Congress Cataloging-in-Publication Data
Beaulieu, John E., 1948-
  Working parents can raise smart kids : the "time-starved" parent's guide to helping your child succeed in school / John Beaulieu , Alex Granzin ; with Deborah S. Romaine -- 1st ed.
    p. cm.
    Includes bibliographical references and index.
    Preassigned LCCN: 98-67442
    ISBN: 0-9666316-5-X

  1. Education--Parent participation. 2. Home and school. I. Granzin, Alex. II. Title.

LB1048.5.B43 1999   *371.192*
                            QBI98-1066

PARKLAND PRESS
11003 A Street South
Tacoma, Washington 98444-0646

BOOK ORDERS ONLY: 1-800-461-0070
ALL OTHER INQUIRIES – CORPORATE OFFICE: 1-253-531-5179

Acknowledgments

We would like to thank the many people who had a part in making this book a reality. First and foremost, our spouses and children. Their help, patience and support were the catalysts that made this project possible.

Many educators and parents gave up valuable time to review the outline and content of this book. We are indebted to the following reviewers: Jonathan Brendefur, Mary Clingan, John Goebel, Janet Kaye, Jan Lewis, Frank Olson, Dan Staffieri, and Shirley Terry. Their comments and suggestions were invaluable in helping us to decide what to include in this book.

We would also like to acknowledge the work of Roxanne Carrington. Her exceptional artistic skills were responsible for the cover design, illustrations and the text layout.

Last, but not least, we would like to thank Phoebe C. Cannell and Metha Weber for their tireless efforts in the proofing and editing of this manuscript.

John E. Beaulieu

Alex Granzin

Deborah S. Romaine

TABLE OF CONTENTS

Introduction

We know how busy your day is. We're working parents ourselves, and we know "free time" is the stuff of dreams. So we've organized this book to fit into the few minutes here and there that you have time to read. Each chapter offers specific suggestions that you can begin using right away. There's no big secret that we've saved until the end, so you don't have to read the whole book before you can start helping your kids do better in school.

What's Different About This Book

As a concerned parent, you've no doubt browsed dozens of books about all aspects of raising a child, from dealing with diaper rash to surviving adolescence. Many contain useful advice – especially if you have nothing to do all day but sit home and practice. But you're a busy working parent, and you barely have time for your life's activities as it is. The last thing you need is another program. Relax. That's the last thing you'll get from this book.

This book is **not** about doing schoolwork with (or for) your child. It's **not** about being an expert in math or reading or spelling or any other school subject. And it's **not** about becoming a teacher. Your child's school employs educated, experienced teachers to teach academics. We believe it's the school's job to educate your child, and your child's job to do the work of learning.

Your job is to be the parent, to provide support and encouragement for your child on his journey of learning. This book **is** about suggesting ways to help your child succeed in school that fit into your lifestyle and the time you have available. It **is** about helping you create a home environment that supports your child's learning. It **is** about interacting with your child every day in ways that can have a more significant effect on your child's school success than you could ever imagine.

As important as academics are, the non-academic skills are critical to school success – responsibility, persistence, and independence, to name a few. Children who are weak in these non-academic skills often struggle in school. This is where you, the parent, have the starring role. Through small steps and little changes, you can achieve big gains in strengthening your child's abilities in these critical areas. Again, we emphasize that these are steps you can fit into your daily activities.

Real life is no cakewalk. We know this. Real life overflows with appointments and meetings and timelines and deadlines and homework and band and sports and… the list goes on and on. Yet no matter how much you have to do in a day, you still have only so much time in which to do it. Too many books offer idealistic advice doomed to fail in the real world because they don't account for, well, real life. We've done our best to write a book based on reality, with the pressures and time constraints of your life in mind. We offer realistic suggestions that working parents can implement. We also will tell you why the skills these suggestions develop and reinforce are critical to school success. And we hope, when you've read a chapter or two, that you realize your role as a parent is just as important to your child's success in school as is the role of your child's teacher.

How to Get the Most From This Book

We wrote the chapters in this book so that you could read them in any order you like. We recommend that you start by browsing through the chapters to pick out the ones you can begin working on within your time constraints. Select any chapter, read it through, and put its concepts into practice. Then choose another chapter and do the same thing. This is no all-or-nothing proposition. It's a series of topics and suggestions for real families with real time challenges. Most chapters end with a concise summary of the chapter's key concepts and the benefits for your child of putting them into practice. References guide you to additional information about topics that interest you beyond what we've covered in this book.

The more ideas you can put into practice, of course, the more effective the results. But incorporating even one or two concepts can make a significant difference in your child's school performance.

Methods That Work

Co-authors John E. Beaulieu, Ph.D. and Alex Granzin, Ph.D., have a combined 45 years of educational experience. The methods we suggest are rooted in this experience, and have been successful with countless children and their parents. But that's not the only way we know they work. We know these methods work because we're working parents, too, and we've used them with our *own* children. Dr. Beaulieu's daughter graduated valedictorian of her high school class, and is now an honors student in college. Dr. Granzin's daughter just graduated an honors student in junior high school. And writer Ms. Romaine, a busy working parent who is *not* a child psychologist and knew little about these methods when she joined Drs. Beaulieu and Granzin in writing this book, has greatly reduced homework hassles and improved the level of responsibility toward schoolwork with her elementary-age children.

You, too, can put these methods to work for your children. No matter how busy you are, you can fit many of our ideas and suggestions into your present schedule. Just choose those that interest you, and have fun trying them out! You'll be pleasantly surprised (and maybe overjoyed) with the results. And you'll enjoy watching your child grow and flourish as he succeeds in school. It's easier than you think. You *can* raise smart kids.

CHAPTER 1

What's a Time-Starved Parent to Do?

If you're like most parents, you care – deeply – about your child's future.

You want to give your child the best possible preparation for a lifetime of learning. You want him to have the best learning opportunities – and of course, the best support you can give to help him take advantage of them.

Sounds great on paper, but how do you make it happen? After all, there's only so much time in each day, and other obligations lay claim to most of yours. The 8-hour workday is as much of a fairy tale as Cinderella. Early meetings, late meetings, and deadlines drain energy. Commuting time and overtime draw minutes and hours from other parts of the day. Meals, laundry, cleaning, and yard work await you at home. From the time the alarm clock rousts you out of bed in the morning till you crash into bed some 16 or 18 hours later, you're on the go.

You, like most working parents, are starved for time. How can you help your child succeed in school when you barely have time to sneeze?

The typical working parent puts in the equivalent of an 80-hour workweek.

■ *The Challenges of Our Changing World*

It's not just your imagination. You really do have less free time than your parents did. Not since the 1920s have Americans worked longer hours and enjoyed less leisure time. If yours is a two-parent home with both parents working full time, you're putting in the equivalent of an additional day and a half of work each week between the two of you. And between job, family and household responsibilities, the typical working parent puts in the equivalent of an 80-hour workweek. Even if you do have a reasonable balance between work and family, you probably still feel like your life flashes by almost before you notice it.

It's more than just the times that have changed. Technology now drives our lives, from computers to cellular phones. This alters not just the present but also the future your child faces. Most new jobs require increasing levels of education and technical proficiency. What your child learns in school today is barely a beginning; learning challenges will continue even after the end of formal schooling. The skills she develops in school and at home *now* will determine how well she meets those challenges later in life.

You can help your child be:

responsible

organized

persistent

cooperative

self-confident

■ *Success Really Does Begin at Home*

Take a moment right now for a slow, deep breath. Maybe two, if it's been one of *those* days. There now, feeling better? Good! Because chances are, if you stop to look at yourself with a more compassionate and objective eye, you'll see a caring, concerned parent who's already doing a pretty good job of raising your child. That you're reading this book demonstrates that you are *interested* in his school and learning experiences; and that is critical to his success in school.

OK. Now, ready for the bombshell? **The most effective ways you can help your child succeed in school have very little to do with schoolwork and academics.** Surprised? Many parents are. Think of your child's education as an ongoing construction project. While her schooling provides the floors and walls, the learning experiences she brings from home form the foundation. The stronger the foundation, the stronger the learning structure. Of course good schools, teachers, books, and learning opportunities are both valuable and important. But when it comes right down to it (and educators will be the first to agree), the child who brings from home a positive attitude and a willingness to learn enters the classroom with a significant advantage.

Your daily activities and interactions with your child offer abundant and important opportunities for you to influence her success or failure as a student. By using your time together more effectively, you can help her develop a more positive attitude toward learning and school, and become more responsible, organized, persistent, cooperative, and self-confident. These essential traits guide your child around obstacles and through challenges, and are critical for her success in school and in life.

Your Child's Role ■

You cannot learn for your child.

You cannot, no matter how much time and energy you dedicate, learn *for* your child. Learning is your child's job. It can't take place unless he does the work himself. Your child must do his homework assignments, read his books, write his reports, and complete his special projects. It is also his job to bring home the books and materials he needs to do his homework, and to take his completed assignments back to school.

Your child's classroom and homework assignments help him learn by doing – something that can happen only when he does the doing. As much as you want to make your child's life easier, you have to let him struggle a bit to figure out tough assignments on his own. When your child works through challenges, he gains a new (and often enlightened) perspective on classroom lessons. He becomes an independent learner.

To truly succeed in learning, however, your child needs a broad variety of skills that extend beyond academics. He must pay attention in class, follow directions, work hard to stretch his capabilities, cooperate with teachers and classmates, and participate with enthusiasm. These are the skills that will determine whether your child succeeds in school, and the skills over which you as a parent have the greatest influence.

Schoolwork and related activities are your child's responsibility.

■ *Your Role*

So what is your job as a caring, concerned parent? It is **not** your role as the parent to write book reports, correct math problems, or leave work in the middle of the morning to deliver forgotten assignments, books, or musical instruments to the classroom. Make this your mantra: **Schoolwork and its related activities are my child's responsibility.** While it's natural to want to rescue your child from situations that create pressure and unpleasantness, rushing in when the situation becomes difficult is more likely to be detrimental than helpful.

It is your job to help your child develop those critical life skills without which no learning can take place. You are the best one to teach the value of education, how to use time efficiently, and how to try hard and persist in the face of difficulty. You don't do this by sitting with your child to do homework. You do this by demonstrating genuine interest in his assignments and progress, developing good relationships with his teacher, structuring a home life that is both educationally stimulating and supportive of his schoolwork, and by demonstrating how important education is to you. These actions support your child's endeavors and help him develop important life skills that prepare him for learning. Your job is not always easy, but it doesn't need to be as hard as it often gets.

When we say it's important to let your child take responsibility for her schoolwork and assignments, we're not suggesting you abandon her to her own devices. To the contrary, we believe the more time you give your child, the greater likelihood her school experiences will be positive and successful. There are, obviously, times when you can't be there with your child. However, you can structure your home environment to support and enhance her learning when you're away. Even with limited time, you can have a profound effect on your child's education.

Even with limited time, you can have a profound effect on your child's education.

The Value of Your Participation ■

Your support is critical to your child's success. Study after study confirms that the single, most influential adult in a child's life is a parent. Your concern and participation as a parent are vital elements of your child's development. When you support and encourage your child, you give her the confidence and the framework to fulfill her capabilities. Without your support and encouragement, her chance to become a successful learner is greatly diminished.

It's not easy to be green, says the most famous of Muppets™, the inimitable Kermit™. It's not easy to be a child, either. Beneath the surface of all that looks like play is the very serious business of preparing for adulthood. Your child needs a guide, mentor, and role model as she makes her way along this journey... she needs you.

WORKING PARENTS CAN RAISE SMART KIDS

Time is an Investment
in Your Child's Future ■

We know you want to give your child the best education possible, to prepare him for a bright and successful future. And we know the time you have to help with this education is limited. Our suggestions are designed to help you make the most of the time you have. As educators and as parents, we encourage you to look for ways to free additional time in your life (look for minutes, not hours or days), and spend that time with your children. You can't make a better investment.

You can't make a better investment than spending time with your children.

You *can* spend time with your child, no matter how time-starved you are. Just as saving ten dollars a week can add up to a sizable nest egg over the years, setting aside a few blocks of time to support your child's learning efforts can make a measurable and significant difference in his education and life. The key is to make the best possible use of the time you and your child spend together.

WORKING PARENTS CAN RAISE SMART KIDS

CHAPTER 2

Ready to Learn

Stand outside your child's classroom for a few minutes in the morning.

Can you pick out the children who are ready to start another day of learning? Probably so, and with ease. They're the ones who are excited and happy as they pull out completed homework assignments and get their books ready. They laugh and talk, clamor for attention from each other and even from the teacher. When the bell rings they jostle and push to get to their seats. They are ready to learn.

You can also pick out the children who start the day at a disadvantage. They drag into the classroom, tired and grumpy. They slide into their seats and slump, head resting on crossed arms, until the bell rings. When the teacher takes attendance, they raise a weary hand long enough to be noticed, then rummage through their desks to locate the books for the morning's first lesson.

■ *The Basics Give the Day a Good Start*

What separates these two groups of children? Quite simply, three essential basics: proper rest, nutrition, and physical activity. Children who have a regular bedtime, do homework before other recreational activities, read and play interactive games instead of watching TV, engage in regular and vigorous physical activity, and eat regular, nutritious meals have a solid foundation to carry them through each day. Though sitting in a classroom all day may not seem that strenuous to us adults, learning requires children to exert incredible effort and concentration. Nutritious meals and snacks, plenty of rest, and physical exercise are three basics that help fuel your child's readiness to learn.

Help Your Child Get Enough Rest

It's a rare household indeed where getting the kids to bed on time happens without challenge. All too often time slips from six o'clock to ten o'clock almost unnoticed, and the kids are still up. Consistency is the best policy for healthy bedtime routines. Even if bedtime hassles rule at your house right now, it's never too late to make changes.

Lights out. Set a time by which you expect your child to be in bed. Each child's need for sleep varies, and often changes, as the child grows older. Most children need between 8 and 10 hours of sleep each night to feel well-rested. Work back from the time your child must get up in the morning to establish a time for bed, taking into consideration what you know about your child's sleeping habits. Try the schedule for two weeks. If he generally falls asleep within 15 or 20 minutes, the time and amount of sleep are probably right. If he is still awake an hour after bedtime, extend "lights out" by half an hour.

Develop Routines That Work

Keep it positive.

Involve your children in the process.

Let your children know when they're making progress.

Be patient.

If your child must get up at ...	5:30 am	6:00 am	6:30 am
Try a bedtime of ...	8:00 pm	8:30 pm	9:00 pm
With preparations starting at ...	7:30 pm	8:00 pm	8:30 pm

Bedtime routines. What your child does before going to bed can make the difference between a child ready to sleep and one determined to resist. Many families find that using the 30 minutes before bedtime to prepare helps children unwind and get ready for sleep. This can be when your child lays out clothes for the next day, gets homework assignments and books ready to go, gets dressed for bed, and completes other bedtime routines such as brushing teeth. Younger children need more guidance and supervision than older ones. Be sensitive to each child's unique needs. One child may take more than 30 minutes for these rituals, while another may spend the last 15 minutes of this time quietly reading before bed. If time seems to slip away despite your best intentions, try setting a timer or an alarm to help all family members remember when it is time to start getting ready for bed – and let nothing interfere.

Rise and shine. Children who get enough sleep wake up more easily in the morning. Having clothes and school things ready the night before takes some of the pressure off the rush to get out the door on time. Allow enough time in the morning for your child to take care of bathroom needs, get dressed, and eat a nutritious breakfast. To get from bed to the door takes most children 45 minutes to an hour.

Making it work. Once you've established bedtimes and routines, talk with your child to be sure she understands what you expect. Involve her in decisions about what preparations she will do and when. Ask her what she would like you to do to help her manage her new routines. You'll have a much easier time implementing routines that your child has helped develop and shape. 'Formalize' your agreement in some fashion – shake hands, hug, write and sign a brief note, or whatever your family does to confirm important agreements.

You'll have a much easier time implementing routines that your children have helped develop and shape.

Be prepared for a few bumps and jolts, even a short detour or two, if this path is new for your family. It's the nature of kids to push their limits, and it's the nature of parents to become frustrated when children don't behave as expected. Resist nagging and yelling when your child pushes to test your resolve. Instead, try countering complaints by asking for suggestions to make adjustments or improvements in the routine. You'll need to monitor new bedtime routines very closely at first, and intermittently after they appear to be well established.

Remain firm about the need for your child to get adequate rest each night. Generally, once she realizes that she does feel better when she's well rested, bedtime will be much easier – and less time-consuming – for the entire family. Bedtime can become a fairly automatic routine, bringing a calm and predictability to the end of the day that all family members can enjoy.

Help Your Child Eat Nutritiously ■

"Three squares a day" was once an American goal. Today, we're lucky to get one full meal in on a busy day – and that often turns out to be fast food. Most of us don't eat poorly because we lack the money to buy nutritious food. Rather, we have come to believe that eating properly takes too much time out of a hectic day already crammed with more demands than we can meet. In reality, however, eating nutritiously takes no more time than eating junk food. Bodies and minds perform best when they are properly fueled.

A good breakfast is a good start. Mornings in many households are rushed and frantic, with family members dashing about to complete necessary preparations for the day. Often the outfit that looked good last night has turned into a horrible costume by daybreak, leading to frantic efforts to find something else to wear. All of a sudden it's time to go – and breakfast becomes the day's first sacrifice. Minimize this chaos with good bedtime routines.

Yet nothing gives the day a better start than a good breakfast. Many studies have shown that children concentrate and perform better in school and on tests when they've had a nutritious breakfast. While few of us have the time or energy to prepare a full meal before the sun comes up, many items can provide a tasty, nutritious start.

Set a healthy, positive example by preparing meals that are low in fat and high in nutrients.

Lunch refuels for the rest of the day.
Buy or pack is a daily dilemma in many households. Buying often wins by default because it's faster and easier. Besides, we reason, school lunches are nutritious because they have to be. Sadly, many school lunch programs offer meals that are low in nutritional value and high in fat and sugar. Regulations only mandate bare minimums. If your child regularly eats school lunches, check the menu each week to see what he's eating. Ask him if he likes the school's food. Ask what he eats and what he throws away.

A bowl of low fat, low sugar cereal with milk provides both simple and complex carbohydrates to deliver instant and long-lasting energy. Add some sliced banana, berries or raisins for added flavor and nutrients.

Low fat yogurt with fruit goes down quickly. Sprinkle on some granola to add crunch and carbohydrates.

Whole grain waffles can go from freezer to toaster to table in less than three minutes — and are especially tasty topped with fresh fruit or applesauce.

For the picky eater or child who just can't eat breakfast foods, there's nothing wrong with leftover pasta dishes, broiled chicken or pizza that are good cold or take only a minute or two in the microwave to warm.

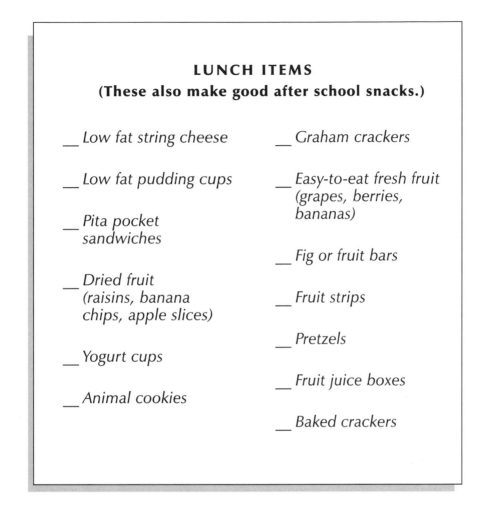

LUNCH ITEMS
(These also make good after school snacks.)

__ *Low fat string cheese*

__ *Low fat pudding cups*

__ *Pita pocket sandwiches*

__ *Dried fruit (raisins, banana chips, apple slices)*

__ *Yogurt cups*

__ *Animal cookies*

__ *Graham crackers*

__ *Easy-to-eat fresh fruit (grapes, berries, bananas)*

__ *Fig or fruit bars*

__ *Fruit strips*

__ *Pretzels*

__ *Fruit juice boxes*

__ *Baked crackers*

Packed lunches often lose out because they take time to prepare. Like anything else, however, this can become just part of the morning routine. While sending nutritious foods to school for your child's lunch doesn't guarantee that she will eat them, there are many appealing choices that require little effort on your part. Let her help choose what to pack.

Set an example when you set the table.
Dinner, or supper, is the meal most
families are likely to share. Use this meal
to set a healthy, positive example by
preparing meals that are low in fat and
high in nutrients. Involve your child in
making food choices. This helps him gain
a "real life" understanding of nutritional
values and differences, as well as learn
what ingredients go into favorite dishes.
Occasional fast food is fine; eating well is
not about depriving yourself of all the
foods you like.

"Power" munching. Many kids, it seems, eat
all the time. Their growing bodies need
plenty of fuel, and their smaller stomachs
may need more frequent filling. Nutritious
snacking can meet these needs without
ruining regular meals. Snacking has come
to be viewed as harmful because typical
snack items – chips, cookies, candy – are
not all that healthy. The easiest way to be
sure that children eat snacks that are good
for them is to be sure there is no junk food
in the house. This has the added benefit of
helping everyone eat better.

The items listed on the previous page as
examples for nutritious lunches also make
good snack foods, as do other foods like
popcorn and rice cakes with fruit spread
or peanut butter. Replace soda pop and
colas, which are often high in sugar and
also contain caffeine, with milk, fruit
juices and even just water.

Take your child grocery shopping with you.
Children enjoy helping to make choices
about what the family will eat. Going grocery
shopping together is a good opportunity for
you to teach your child how to read package
labels for nutritional information, select
fresh produce, and plan meals. She's more
likely to eat what she's helped select.

Exercise Keeps the Body and the Mind Fit

Most kids play hard, which gives them the
exercise their growing bodies need to
develop strength and coordination. Even
recess can be quite a workout for children
who run and swing and climb. Organized
sports provide healthy physical activity
as well as important social interaction.
Exercise channels and burns excess energy,
helping children feel alert and ready to learn
in the classroom.

The risk of passive replacements. Many
activities compete for your child's time and
attention. Two that warrant particular
discussion are television and video games.
These passive forms of entertainment do not
engage either the mind or the body. Limit
TV watching and video game playing to
encourage your child to get the physical
activity she needs. (Chapter 10, *Learning
and Television*, provides more on this
topic.)

What's good for your child is good for the whole family. Your family's health overall is very important. Even if you've slipped into less than desirable habits, you can still make healthy changes. Kids seldom have any trouble figuring out when the adults in their lives say one thing and do another. It's much easier to draw your child from the TV or video game for some outside activity if physical exercise is a regular part of your life, too. When you catch your child making healthy choices, compliment him. Let him know he's made a good decision, and that you noticed.

Look for activities the entire family can enjoy together, like bicycling, hiking, swimming, skiing, inline or roller-skating, tennis, badminton, baseball, volleyball – even just walking. In addition to getting in better shape, you'll all get to know each other better. And who knows, you could just end up having some fun together!

CHAPTER CONCEPTS

- Proper rest
- Bedtime routines
- Importance of breakfast
- Physical activity

- Good nutrition
- Power munching
- Learn by shopping

BENEFITS & RESULTS

YOUR CHILD:

…is alert, attentive, ready to learn –
and "just feels better."

…has better test scores,
better grades, better concentration.

…has energy to meet the demands of learning.

…is more likely to complete homework –
has the strength to do homework at the end of the day.

…is ready to start the day organized.

…is more likely to follow agreed-upon routines.

…learns about good nutrition.

PLUS:

There are fewer family hassles in the morning.

There are fewer hassles at bedtime.

Parents' well-being improves.

You may find more time to spend with your child.

CHAPTER 3

Building Positive Attitudes Toward School

How would you describe a child who has a positive attitude toward school and learning?

Most parents would say such a child heads to school with enthusiasm, eager for another day of learning, and comes home bubbling with stories of the day's adventures. He asks a lot of questions, enjoys working on school projects, and makes a good effort to get his homework done. Most teachers would say this child participates energetically in classroom discussions and activities. He determinedly grapples with new ideas and works through challenges. He cooperates with teachers and classmates, and makes good use of independent work periods.

Such children are not imaginary. They thrive in every classroom in every school. In fact, odds are high that you've got one or more living in your home, even if presently in rough form.

■ *Start Young*

Positive attitudes are easiest to shape when you encourage them from an early age. Begin by showing your child that learning is fun. Read to her, and later read together *with* her. Play games together. Watch television programs with educational value, and talk about what you learn. Let her see that you, too, learn new things every day. Create surroundings that provide a rich learning environment. (See Chapter 4, *Furnishing Your Home for Learning*.) Take family outings to interesting and stimulating places like museums, historic sites, state and national landmarks, and other locations that help your child connect "book" learning with real life experiences.

No matter what your child's age, it's never too late to shape positive attitudes. Obviously, if you have an older child whose attitude toward school is less than positive, you have some work to do. But with persistence and consistency, you can begin to change his attitude toward school and learning. Not only is his school performance likely to improve, but also his (and your) home life. When your child has a positive attitude toward school and learning, he comes home happier, gives you less grief over homework and school projects, seldom has school problems, and generates less family tension. Your child's positive attitude clearly creates a win-win situation.

The Power of Your Influence ■

Who do you think influences your child the most? Look no further than the mirror. Your child's interest in school is often a reflection of your own. If you value education and hold learning in high regard, chances are your child will, too. Whether she acknowledges it or not, your child looks to you when she forms her own values and opinions. *You* are the most significant influence on your child's attitude toward school. If you remain positive about learning even in the face of challenge, so will she.

Kids need real life connections to show them that education delivers.

■ *Show Your Child How Learning is Important in Your Life*

Take advantage of the natural opportunities that come up to show your child how education, both formal and informal, remains a major factor in your life and in your profession or career. Was there a teacher who in some way changed your life? A skill learned in school that has made a difference? If so, tell your child about it. Are you learning something new? A musical instrument, a foreign language, advanced skills for your job? Let your child see your efforts, persistence, and successes. Most importantly, let your child see that you enjoy learning new things. Share how much fun it is to do something once you've learned more about it – how a golf clinic improved your game, how an advanced class gave you knowledge in a special interest, or even how a job-related workshop made your job easier. Kids need real life connections to show them that education delivers.

Sharing your challenges and successes can provide support and encouragement – as long as you keep the tone of your conversations casual. Your child shouldn't feel threatened or singled out every time you start talking about education. As soon as you start sounding like a lecture, you've lost his interest. Make sure your points fit naturally into the discussion, and keep your comments relevant. Remember that it's nearly impossible for your child to imagine you at his age, struggling to master cursive writing and long division. Your child should see your educational experiences as a part of you, not as a trumped-up presentation.

All too often, children come to view learning as something they get to stop doing when they become adults. You want your child to see that learning is a lifelong, and pleasurable, adventure, not just hear you talk about it. Actions always speak louder than words – and you know your child watches what you do. This kind of sharing with your child can have an enormous impact on her education, yet can take place naturally, without much extra effort or time from you.

Your child should see that learning is a lifelong, and pleasurable, adventure.

Keep a Positive Tone About School and Teachers ■

What was the last thing your child heard you say about her school or teacher? If your comments were complimentary and positive, pat yourself on the back. If you criticized or complained, go stand in the corner. Nothing garners your child's full and undivided attention like a conflicting message. If you tell your child that education and school are important and then put down the teacher, which message do you want him to remember? Which one do you think he will remember? Negatives, sadly, stick with us longer.

Refrain from criticisms and negative comments about school and teachers when your child might hear you. No matter how valid your concerns, expressing them in front of her will not resolve them. If your disagreement is strong and you cannot present your views without sounding critical, hold your tongue. It's fine to let your child know that you disagree with a teacher or the school on a certain issue. Just do it in a way that expresses the disagreement in terms of an action (rather than a person) and with respect. "There are many ways to do that group science project. Mr. Chapman is a capable teacher, and I'm sure he has his reasons for wanting you to do it as he assigned."

Despite claims to the contrary, your child both needs and wants your interest.

Negative messages about school and teachers can undo everything you've done to help your child build and maintain positive attitudes about school.

■ *Talk With Your Child About School*

Ask your child about school... every day. You can initiate these discussions during times you and your child are already together, such as during dinner, while riding in the car, or just before bed. You might set aside a few minutes each day just to talk. Open with a basic invitation, "tell me about something you did at school today." If that returns the typical abbreviated response kids are prone to deliver, keep probing. Ask about an assignment, a test, the lunch menu, recess, the teacher – anything to get your child talking.

Don't worry if your child gives brief answers or resists the conversation altogether. Kids can put parents on a pretty lean diet when it comes to giving out information about school. You may have to prod, pry, wheedle and cajole just to find out what was on the lunch menu! As frustrating as this can be, take heart – your efforts mean more to your child than she lets on. Your questions tell her that you care, even if they seldom generate the detailed responses you'd like to hear. Despite claims to the contrary, she both needs and wants your interest. **Keep asking, because that tells your child you care about her education and what's going on at school.**

So how do you keep this up without driving both of you crazy? Again, stay casual. Don't turn the situation into a drill. Keep your comments positive. Resist the urge to respond with judgmental statements. Over time, your child will know that you're going to keep asking, whether he responds or not.

Your questions tell your child that you care.

Ask Specific Questions ■

Sometimes kids don't say much because they're not sure what you want to know. Make your questions specific. This shows a more genuine interest, and confirms that you've been paying attention in earlier conversations. It also increases the number and quality of informational tidbits your child will toss you.

Some specific questions might include:

- "How was today's math lesson in fractions?"
- "What did you do today on your science project with Lynn and Robert?"
- "What did Mrs. Simmons say about your book report?"
- "How was the discussion about the story you read for English class?"
- "Did you watch the film about the nervous system today in health class?"

Respond to your child's answers with additional specific questions, if you want to know more. Just keep the tone informal. You don't have to know every detail of your child's day to stay in touch with his school activities and progress.

Resist the temptation to talk more than you listen.

■ Be Ready to Listen

Pay attention when your child starts talking to you, even if she doesn't seem to be taking the conversation very seriously. When you are listening, give – and be sure she knows she has – your full attention. Look at her when she speaks. Make eye contact. Children are quick to conclude that "no one ever listens to me!" – be careful not to give them any reason to think so. Resist the temptation to talk more than you listen. While dialogue is a two-way process, you want your child to feel comfortable talking to you – she already spends a lot of time listening.

If your child starts talking about one thing and then darts off in another direction, be patient. Adults tend to grow restless with such wanderings in children, because we feel we have better things to do with our time than listen to odd little stories. *Get to the point!* we silently (and sometimes not so silently) implore. And this is where adults tend to go astray, because those wanderings *are* the point. Remember that these talks with your child are not inquisitions. The point is to develop a comfortable relationship that allows him to feel comfortable talking with you. Marisa's lost necklace, Justin's three-point basket in gym class, Kaleema and Stephanie teaming at recess to keep Cassandra off the tire swing, Keith copying Moira's math answers – these details matter to your child, at least for the moment, so they should matter to you.

Let your conversations with your child take their natural course. In all likelihood, they will be short because the time you have together has boundaries. This is OK. Over time the pieces will fit together, and the meanderings will begin to reveal a more complete picture of your child's daily school experiences.

■ *Leave Room for Feelings*

Let your child express her feelings about school. Don't argue, or be too quick to express concern. If she greets your question about how a math assignment went with "Math stinks!" your first inclination might be to launch into a lecture about the importance of math skills. A more neutral response – "I'm sorry you're struggling with those problems" – acknowledges your child's feelings and permits her to freely express them. This requires patience and attentiveness on your part. Respond positively and with praise for specific answers. Show that you understand and accept her point of view, though you don't have to agree with it. Again, neutral or reflective comments are a good approach.

- "Team projects can sometimes be challenging when some team members do more work than others. I'm sorry to hear that Lynn is not pulling her load."

- "I can almost see the smile that was on your face when you went to the board and wrote the correct answer, Jeff. I bet that made you feel pretty good!"

- "You completed two extra reading charts this month, Sally. I'm proud of the extra effort you've put into improving your reading skills."

Everyone has bad days, so relax a bit when your child has his. Unless every day is a bad day, your child's unhappiness with a particular project or assignment has little to do with his overall attitude toward school and learning.

Ask to See Your Child's Schoolwork ■

Ask to see your child's schoolwork on a regular basis. Praise good work and effort. Point out progress. Share successes with other family members. You might post papers on the refrigerator or family bulletin board. Let your child overhear you telling others how proud of him you are, and what a good job he's doing with his schoolwork. And when he makes a significant effort or achievement, give him extra recognition. Share your child's excitement about outstanding papers, major school projects, school awards, and other special work.

Kids who participate in school activities have a more positive attitude toward school.

Encourage Participation in Activities Beyond the Classroom ■

Kids who participate in school activities beyond the classroom have a more positive attitude toward school. When your child participates in chorus, band, chess club, computer club, sports, and other activities, she develops a sense of belonging and self-confidence that often carries over into the classroom. Many of these activities carry over into academics. Chess teaches analytical skills and strategy, for example, and sports emphasize teamwork. Music, drama and dance help your child "experience" the classics she learns about in class. Scouts, clubs, and youth organizations support her social development. Extracurricular activities show her that learning can take place in fun and interesting ways. Your child sees that her school offers meaning in her life beyond the classroom.

■ Encourage Your Child to Develop Hobbies and Special Interests

Hobbies often provide opportunities to develop school-related skills. Your child learns to follow directions independently, organize materials and information, and apply reading, and other academic skills to activities he enjoys. Hobbies encourage him to continue learning beyond the classroom.

Even small volunteer efforts show your child that your commitment to her education is sincere.

■ Participate in School Events

If you're telling your child how important school is, yet you're too tired to attend open houses, parent-teacher conferences, or volunteer for school events, what message are you really sending? Your child will quickly determine that your talks about the importance of school are just that – talk.

Most kids enjoy having their parents participate in school events. At the very least, attend open houses and parent-teacher conferences. These activities let you see where your child spends most of her waking hours and help you establish a relationship with your child's teacher. When possible, volunteer to help out at your child's school. Even small volunteer efforts show your child that your commitment to her education is sincere. Does your job keep you too busy to break away for field trips? Talk with your employer about short stints volunteering in the classroom. Many employers support community involvement efforts like tutoring of reading, for example, by allowing employees to take an extended lunch one day a week. Chapter 7, *Developing a Partnership With Your Child's School*, offers more suggestions about how to become involved with your child's school even when your time is limited.

Letting your child miss school for a family vacation sends the message that fun is more important than school.

Keep Your Child in School ■

What do your actions say to your child about the importance of education? Today's busy life-styles favor short vacations over long weekends, intensifying the temptation to leave early and return late. Resist! Nothing helps your child keep up with his lessons like being in school when he is supposed to be there. Letting him miss school, even just a day or two, for a family vacation sends a powerful message that fun is more important than school. If you must pull your child from classes early, make arrangements to get his assignments in advance. Have him complete them on a daily basis just as he would if he were in class.

Health care needs pose a similar concern. Most of the time your child's needs are routine – eye exams, dental cleanings, physical exams. Unless your child is ill enough to be out of school anyway, try to schedule routine health care appointments around school hours.

■ *Positive Attitudes Build Strong Foundations*

The more your child sees school as a positive experience, the more likely it is that he will enjoy academic and social success. Your efforts and encouragement – now, while he is forming his learning foundation – can go a long way toward building positive images about school and learning.

CHAPTER CONCEPTS

- Read to and with your child.
- Take family outings to stimulating places.
- Show your child how learning has helped you.
- Talk with your child about a significant teacher in your life.
- Let your child see you learning something.
- Talk positively about school and teachers.
- Ask your child something about school every day.
- Encourage your child to have hobbies.

BENEFITS & RESULTS

YOUR CHILD:

…tries harder.

…participates eagerly in the classroom.

…cooperates with teachers and classmates.

…is a better independent worker.

…completes homework with fewer problems.

…is happier.

…has fewer problems in school.

…sees the connection between school and life.

…knows how much you value education.

…earns better grades and test scores.

PLUS:

Your home life improves.

CHAPTER 4

Furnishing Your Home for Learning

For kids, life's a game.

Play is the most important element of their lives, and they play hard. Learning is part of that play. Problem is, adults don't often see it that way. *Stop playing around*, we scold. Yet children learn best when they're having fun. With a little thought and planning, you can furnish your home with activities kids enjoy. They won't even know they're learning!

■ *What's in a Game of Monopoly®?*

There they are, your kids and a couple of their friends, sprawled on the living room floor. A Monopoly® board lies in the center of their irregular circle. They've been playing for hours; you can hear their shouts and laughter (and occasional arguments) clear in the kitchen. Are they wasting time, or is something more meaningful taking place? Watch for a few minutes, and you may find yourself pleasantly surprised.

What's in a Game of Monopoly®?

Money management.

Decision-making.

Math skills.

Reading skills.

Popular with all ages, Monopoly® is a classic game of strategy. The object is to "monopolize" ownership of the properties on the board. Each player receives the same amount of money when the game begins, and starts from the same place. The game ends when one player owns enough property to bankrupt the other players. Success combines a little luck and several important skills.

Money management. Children playing Monopoly® decide what they can afford to buy. They collect a salary each time they go around the board, and plan whether to save or spend. They pay taxes and fines. Since they collect rent from players who land on properties they own and pay rent when they land on another player's properties, children have to determine which properties give the best return for their purchase price. Luxury properties have steep purchase prices and high upgrading expenses, but can bankrupt other players in just a round or two. Common properties are cheap to buy and improve, though may take quite a few rounds to deplete the resources of other players.

Decision-making skills. Like life in the real world, Monopoly® is full of options. Buy or pass? Trade or mortgage? Upgrade from houses to hotels? Is it better to own properties in the centers of each block, or at the corners? The decisions involved require risk analysis, negotiation, and strategy. Children learn from their own playing experiences as well as from watching other children play.

Math skills. Effective money management requires strong math skills. Children must be able to quickly add and subtract to make payments and change. Rental values change according to a property's development, and some charge rent according to a roll of the dice. This requires basic multiplication skills. Is it cheaper to pay a flat income tax or a percentage of your worth? The correct decision relies on some quick calculations. Even children too young to have in-depth math skills practice adding the dots on the dice and counting the number of spaces to move.

Reading skills. Some turns result in Community Chest or Chance cards that give instructions. Property cards contain information about rental rates and the costs of making improvements by adding houses or hotels. And of course, the game moves more smoothly when at least one player can read the rules to settle disputes!

To help you start building your library of games, the appendix lists 90 common games that have educational value.

The list includes the educational skills each game develops or reinforces.

■ *Other Games,*
Other Learning Opportunities

Monopoly® is certainly not the only game that supports learning. Many other childhood favorites do so as well. Games like Scrabble®, Clue® and Risk® help develop and reinforce skills in vocabulary and spelling, language, math, memory and recall, deductive reasoning, strategy, and problem solving. Early childhood games like Chutes & Ladders® and Concentration® help children with counting, sequencing, memory, estimating and prediction, and matching.

There are hundreds of games that put classroom skills to use in fun ways that appeal to your child's play-oriented view of life. Seldom will you hear your child complain "This game is too hard, I'll never learn how to play it!" or "Do I have to play this game again?" Learning comes naturally. Children begin to connect school lessons with everyday life, which is an essential step in their intellectual growth and development.

Games aren't the only option. There are hundreds of other items you can have in your home which can help your child practice and reinforce skills learned in school.

These activities and items ...	Help your child ...
Board games, card games, books, children's dictionary, children's magazines, crossword puzzles, puzzle books and brain twisters, journals and diaries for children to write in, computer.	**Practice learned skills**
Board games, puzzle books and brain twisters, measuring and other tools, computer, hobby-related items.	**Develop problem-solving skills**
Art supplies (crayons, chalk, pens, paints, pencils, clay, glue, scissors, craft supplies), musical instruments (drums, tambourine, maracas, recorder, ukulele, guitar, harmonica), cooking utensils (pots, pans, spoons, measuring spoons and cups), old clothes and hats for dress-up, puppets, video camera and film, magnets, magnifying glass, telescope, microscope.	**Explore and create**
Children's encyclopedias, hobby-related items, computer, books, children's magazines, world atlas, state and city maps, educational toys.	**Expand knowledge base**
Clay, yo-yo, jump rope, roller or ice skates, balls, bicycle, pens and pencils, scissors, coloring books, baseball bat and glove, Frisbee®, tetherball, basketball and hoop, building toys.	**Develop motor skills**

■ *Books, Books, Books!*

Fill your home with books! Study after study indicates that children who read well learn faster and do better in school. Kids are never too young or too old for a good story. Read to your child, and have her read to you. Reading to young children helps them develop the language skills they need to become fluent readers themselves. Parents, siblings, grandparents and other relatives, and caregivers can – and should – participate in reading activities. Read bedtime stories to ease the transition from a busy day to a restful night. Read in the car to break the monotony of long or routine trips. Set aside a time each day where family members can take turns reading.

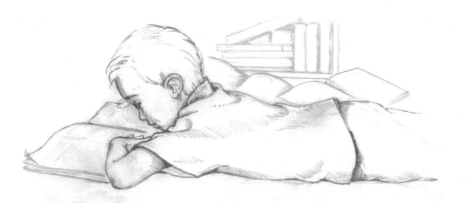

Create a Home Library ■

Develop a broad collection of reading material. Find graded reading lists in school and public libraries.

Storybooks that come with read-along cassette tapes are a wonderful way to introduce young children to reading. Books on computer CD-ROM provide a more interactive experience, allowing your child to participate in the story and practice reading skills. Plastic letters, or blocks with letters on them, help young children learn to shape the words they hear into words they can see. Coloring books based on the alphabet or simple single words combine a favorite activity with learning letters. Similar items with numbers provide practice in sequencing and counting.

Develop a broad collection of reading material for older children. Include many kinds of writing, both fiction and nonfiction. Magazines and newspapers take your child beyond his neighborhood to happenings in other cities, states and countries. Comic books appeal to a child's sense of fun. A good encyclopedia set puts a world of information at your child's fingertips. Novels and short stories indulge his sense of fantasy and imagination. Age-appropriate literary classics introduce writings that you (and your parents before you) enjoyed when you were young. Coloring books that tell stories help your child give shape to the images his imagination generates.

Encourage your child to build her own library. Most schools offer regular opportunities for children to order reasonably priced quality books through special services such as the Scholastic Book Club®. Bookstores usually have children's sections, and many communities have bookstores that specialize in material for children. Stores selling secondhand or used books, garage and yard sales, and library sales are excellent opportunities to pick up good books at bargain prices.

Books make wonderful gifts. Start a family tradition by making a book a part of every birthday and other gift-giving holidays your family celebrates, and reading them together. Helping your child choose and buy her own books has advantages, too. Such participation helps your child develop a sense of ownership and improves the likelihood that he will read the books in his library – not just once, but again and again.

The Public Library ■

Don't overlook your local public library. Most allow patrons, including children, to check out a large number of books at one time. This is an excellent way for your child to sample different kinds of reading material she (or you) might not want to invest in without being certain the interest is there. Though obviously you can't keep library books forever, they offer an inexpensive way to keep a large and varied stock of children's books on hand. As a secondary benefit, using the library provides experience in sharing resources and taking responsibility for borrowed items.

A Quiet Place to Read ■

Your child needs a quiet place to read, a place free from distractions and interruptions so he can fully absorb the book's content and meaning. Schools often use beanbag chairs or soft cushions where a child can relax and be comfortable. You could try something similar in your child's bedroom or another place in your house where there is not a lot of other activity (and NOT in a room where there is a television!). Does your home have a time-worn sofa or easy chair that has been banished to a rec room or study? Chances are this would make a cozy reading retreat. A younger child might enjoy a big cardboard box carved into a "reading house" that is his alone. It's also good to have an area where several family members can gather to read together.

■ *The Home Computer*

Of the many gifts technology has given us, none has been more influential than the personal computer. This is particularly true in education, where computers shape your child's learning experiences from the time she enters preschool. Students learn to write basic book reports using the computer as early as second or third grade. By fifth or sixth grade, teachers expect students to submit papers and reports done by computer. Most schools have computer labs featuring software for students in all grade levels. Many have personal computers in the classroom to broaden the resources available to supplement lessons.

The personal computer passed a milestone in 1996 when it became the first electronic device to outsell the television. Homes with personal computers have outnumbered those without ever since. With a little planning, a computer can be an exciting learning center in your home for all family members.

The "Right" Computer ■

A hallmark of our society is our penchant for the latest and greatest technology. Nothing is good enough unless there's nothing better. The truth is, it's impossible to stay current with computer technology. The next generation of the whiz-bang system you buy today is already in design if not production before the ink dries on your check. With such rapid evolution, how do you know which of today's bells and whistles will be tomorrow's essentials?

Personal computers are software-driven. Items like sound cards, modems, and CD-ROM drives were once options that were nice to have but not necessary. As more programs started taking advantage of the capabilities these options offered, they migrated from nice-to-have to must-have. As a general guideline, the "right" computer for your child and your family is the one that runs the programs you want to use. If you already have a computer in your home, can it run your favorites? Can it run the programs you want to add? If so, your computer is probably right for your family's needs.

Are you buying a new computer system, either as your family's first or a replacement for an outdated one? Talk with several vendors and evaluate different brands before making your decision. Talk with your child's school about the computers used there. Talk to your child about her preferences, consider your budget, and give some thought to how your family will share this resource. Be sure the systems you're considering include everything you'll need to run the programs you want to use, such as a sound card and speakers or a modem. When you've narrowed your choices to two or three, do some reading. Numerous publications compare and rate computer systems.

Computer games can drain your child's time and energy.

■ Beware the "Educational" Computer Game!

There's no doubt that many games, computer as well as the board games mentioned earlier in this chapter, present wonderful opportunities for learning. The interest today's parents have in using the personal computer for educational purposes has not been lost on the computer software companies that compete fiercely for a share of this marketing gold mine, however.

In a broad sense, nearly every computer game could be considered educational. For the most part, computer games reinforce strategy, timing and hand-to-eye coordination. Most involve some level of reading (instructions), and some require basic math skills (scorekeeping). However, studies show that kids retain very little of the "educational" content of these games. This is not exactly what most parents have in mind when they think educational!

Many educational programs, particularly those that target younger children, use a game-oriented approach to make learning fun. This is fine as long as learning, rather than the game, is the ultimate objective. If it is not, your valuable investment becomes a game arcade. While games can be useful rewards for completing studies and assignments, they can also drain your child's time and energy.

Most educational software targets specific age groups and skill needs. Your child's school is a good place to start your software search. What programs does the school use? What programs has the school tried and abandoned? What programs would your child's teacher like to see students use at home? Your local public library is a good place to locate additional resources to help you with your search. Parenting magazines often test and review new programs. Some libraries have computer centers with educational software available for children to use. Many computer stores have demonstration centers where customers can "test-drive" all kinds of software. Your effort up-front will save you time and money in the long run. Once you open a software package, it's yours for keeps whether you like it or not.

> *Schools are a great place to start searching for computer software.*

Don't overlook reference material. There are many fine collections available on CD-ROM that bring research to life for your child through interactive multimedia. CD-ROM encyclopedias include sound clips and movies, animated graphs and displays, and many other features to make learning fun and exciting.

Kids can get help with homework assignments and research reports on the Internet.

■ *Online Resources*

One reason for the personal computer's popularity is its ability to let users literally travel the world without ever leaving home. Online services and the Internet offer additional and extensive access to vast resources, including sites where kids can get help with homework assignments and research reports. Through the Internet, your child can visit libraries, museums, universities, research centers, government agencies, and other locations around the world. (See Appendix II, *Good Websites for Kids*.)

A large number of public and business services permit direct dial access to internal computer systems, sometimes called "bulletin boards," to send or receive information. Your local public library may offer this service to patrons who hold valid library cards. A telephone connection links your home computer with the library's computer system to search reference databases and reserve materials. Some school libraries, particularly those at colleges and universities, offer similar access.

All online connections require a home computer with a modem to connect to a telephone line. Some may also require special software.

Encourage Your Child to Use the Learning Opportunities Your Home Offers ■

Your child will use many of the items in your home without much prompting or assistance from you. Others require a push start from an older sibling or a parent for your child to get going.

Complex games. Can you remember the first few times you played Monopoly®, or Scrabble®, or Clue®? Many favorite childhood games have complex rules and procedures that, while they're second nature to those who already know how to play, are daunting for those just learning. Despite your child's determination when it comes to figuring out such games, guidance from an older sibling or a parent makes the learning more fun. Encourage older siblings to be patient and supportive rather than competitive until the younger child becomes a competent player. It may be necessary for other players to read instructions and other materials to children whose reading skills are still basic.

Hobbies. Hobbies present a wonderful way for children to follow interests awakened through classroom lessons and other learning experiences. A child intrigued by geography or other cultures might enjoy collecting stamps or coins, for example. Building models might appeal to a child who enjoys knowing how things work. Rock collecting could capture the imagination of a child who's always out digging in the yard. Opportunities abound to turn a child's interests into lifelong hobbies. Like complex games, however, hobbies require guidance and assistance. Again, patience and encouragement are key in cultivating your child's efforts. Praise those efforts, not just their results, and keep in touch with your child's activities.

Pull the Plug on Passive Time-Wasters ■

Some common items can easily become distractions that keep your child from getting the most out of the learning environment you've worked so hard to create. Particular time-gobblers include television, telephone and computer games that are entertainment rather than learning-oriented. These passive pastimes do little more than pass the time – time your child could use to enjoy more engaging and productive activities.

Go ahead, you can do it – turn off the TV, limit telephone calls and restrict computer games! Your child won't die from boredom, or even faint. He'll find other ways to entertain himself in the learning-rich environment your home supports.

Time-gobblers:

Television

Telephone

Computer games

Get Involved ■

As a working parent, you have precious little time to spare. Try to find ways to share what you can with your kids. They – and you – will enjoy the results. Mutual interests and hobbies offer ideal opportunities to spend time together. If your life gives you blocks of time that you measure in minutes rather than hours, be creative. Fifteen minutes is long enough to shoot a few hoops, glue the wings on a model airplane, play a duet, or lose a game of checkers.

In the end, it's how you spend your time together that matters. If you spend your time engaged in activities that support your child's interests, you're helping her learn, grow and develop.

■ *Approach Your Home's Learning Environment as Something Dynamic*

An environment that fosters your child's learning is one that grows and changes as do his abilities and interests. Use birthdays and other holidays that your family celebrates as opportunities to purchase items to enhance your home's learning environment, and encourage other family members (including grandparents, aunts, and uncles) to do the same. Some families swap items with others whose children are at different age and skill levels. Garage and rummage sales are often good places to pick up items that will please both your child and your budget.

CHAPTER CONCEPTS

- Use games to enhance learning.
- Use common home items to promote learning.
- Use birthday and holiday purchases to develop learning.
- Create a home library.
- Realize the value of a quiet reading space.
- Make the most of a home computer.
- Go online for learning.
- Develop interests through hobbies.

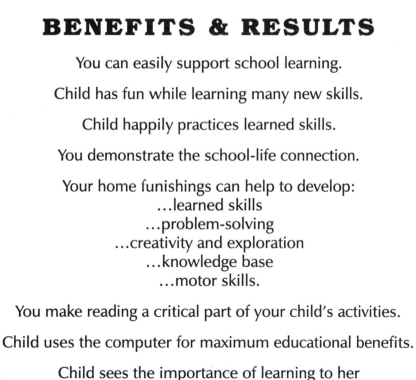

BENEFITS & RESULTS

You can easily support school learning.

Child has fun while learning many new skills.

Child happily practices learned skills.

You demonstrate the school-life connection.

Your home funishings can help to develop:
...learned skills
...problem-solving
...creativity and exploration
...knowledge base
...motor skills.

You make reading a critical part of your child's activities.

Child uses the computer for maximum educational benefits.

Child sees the importance of learning to her
current everyday life.

CHAPTER 5

Opportunities to Learn: Making the Best Use of Available Time

Where are you going to find the time?

Do you often wonder where you're going to find the time to keep up with the endless demands of your busy life, let alone make time to do anything educational with your child? Fortunately, many natural opportunities occur every day for you to weave learning experiences into regular activities. One of the easiest is to include your child in what you're doing. This lets her practice what she's learned in school and makes her feel like an important member of your family. You spend time with your child, she learns new ways to use the knowledge she acquires in school — it's a perfect match!

■ *Everyday Activities Help Your Child Practice and Refine Skills by Doing*

Your home offers a unique opportunity for your child to practice many skills on an individual basis, either independently or by sharing in activities with you. While it might slow you a bit to have a partner in household chores and routine tasks such as cleaning, cooking, sewing, laundry, and gardening, he learns valuable new and "real life" applications for school lessons.

Have your child accompany you when you go grocery shopping, for example, to understand and practice money management and relative value concepts. Product labels and prices give practice in reading, math (serving size per container), and reasoning (comparative value of different brands). Let her help you with routine car maintenance such as filling the washer fluid reservoirs and checking tire air pressure to practice math (measurement) and reading (labels and instructions) skills.

Remember that your child's abilities will grow over time, and your patience will encourage that growth. Children quickly become frustrated when challenges are difficult. It is important to find ways for your child to participate that are within his capabilities. Keep the tone light. After all, he should feel satisfied and successful as a result of sharing tasks and chores with you, not frustrated and incapable. Some day these shared experiences may turn into real help!

Find ways for your child to participate that are within his capabilities.

Choose Family Activities That Promote Learning ■

Many family activities are both fun and educational. Trips to museums and historical sites give your child a sense of perspective about her life experiences. County and state fairs feature displays and events to help broaden her perceptions of her world. Concerts, musical events, and theater presentations expose your child to social and cultural settings. Hikes in the woods and trips to the zoo provide natural opportunities for her to learn about her place in the ecosystem.

Games provide excellent opportunities both for families to spend time together and to reinforce essential learning skills. Games need not be "educational" to promote learning. Almost any game can become an opportunity to support and strengthen thinking skills. Word games provide practice in reading and spelling. Board games often emphasize strategic thought and planning. Jigsaw puzzles allow your child to understand and visualize spatial relationships. Appendix I, *Educational Games*, and Chapter 4, *Furnishing Your Home for Learning,* give more information about how to choose appropriate games.

■ *Make Reading a Family Activity*

Until your child is a fluent reader, you or someone else must read to him every day. Once he can read to himself, read to or with your child whenever time permits. Read to younger children at bedtime. Try to establish a regular family reading time when you can come together to read books that interest everyone. This time need not be lengthy. Just 10 to 15 minutes a day (one or two books) often works fine for younger children. As children grow up, read longer books in short segments (a chapter or two) over several evenings. Family members can take turns choosing books to read. Sometimes you might want to ask your child what he liked and didn't like about the book or story. Can he predict what will happen next? When reading is a family activity, it becomes a regular part of your child's routine. He learns that reading can take him on wonderful adventures. Of course, regular reading also helps your child develop and practice memory, reasoning, and language skills. But he doesn't need to know that! He just needs to know that reading is fun.

When reading is a family activity, it becomes a regular part of your child's routine.

Talk **With** *Your Child* ■

This is not the same as talking *to* your child. Talking *with* your child requires interaction and exchange, which in turn exercises those vital reasoning, thinking and language skills. It also implies mutual interest in, and respect for, each other's thoughts and ideas. Opportunities to talk with your child occur frequently each day — quite literally, any time you are together. Listen to your child's thoughts or opinions without judgment, and permit non-response as well.

Family activities create ideal circumstances for conversation and discussion. Make such discussions part of your regular activities, not just events that occur in times of crisis or trouble. Don't know where to start? You and your child can talk about ...

- Places you've been and things you've done as a family.

- Plans for future family activities.

- Television shows or movies you watch together. You can discuss general themes, character motives, or any other aspects you find interesting.

- Events and issues in the news.

- Important decisions that affect most or all family members.

"Real" conversation is a powerful tool to help your child develop language and vocabulary skills. Best of all, regular dialogue strengthens your relationship and maintains open lines of communication.

Take Advantage of Other Opportunities ■

Your day is filled with opportunities for your child to use and practice newly developed skills. Preparing a recipe for dinner? She can measure and practice important math skills, or read the recipe to you and practice critical reading and comprehension skills. There are dozens of ways your child can learn by helping. Just remember that her participation should be light-hearted, fun, and appropriate for her interests and level of expertise. Here are just a few of the many ways to integrate essential learning skills into everyday activities.

Reading.
Your child could read ...

- lists, notes, and messages.

- a recipe for you or other family member who is cooking.

- the menu when you eat out, and package labels when you go shopping.

- billboards and signs as you are driving.

- directions to new places.

- instructions for assembling a new toy or other item.

- to a younger family member or you as a form of entertainment.

Writing.
Your child could write ...

- notes, messages, and lists containing information you provide, such as reminders to stop at the grocery store on the way home from school and the shopping list of items to buy.

- labels for storage containers and other items.

- letters to friends and relatives.

- thank you notes for gifts and kindnesses.

- notes, lists and short letters for younger siblings.

Math.
Your child can practice math skills through ...

- counting activities, such as how many spoons are in the drawer or red cars on the drive to school.

- keeping score during games.

- measuring activities, such as in following recipes or simple construction projects.

- money management activities, such as counting change or figuring out what combination of bills and coins a price requires.

- telling time, timing things, and figuring out "what time it will be when" (for example, what time a batch of cookies will finish baking).

Language, thinking and reasoning.
Your child can practice these essential communication skills through ...

- exchanging ideas with other family members.

- participating in family decisions.

- explaining things to younger siblings.

- discussing how or why things happen, such as why the days get shorter in winter and longer in summer, or how a light bulb works.

- doing simple word puzzles and anagrams.

It doesn't take much imagination to see that opportunities to help your child learn and practice skills are unlimited. Go ahead, make your own list!

■ *You Already Spend a Lot of Time with Your Child*

You and your child already spend a significant amount of time together, even if only in small chunks scattered throughout the day. Of course, you don't want to structure every minute of your day. Attempting to do so would surely push you over the edge! But you can make more conscious choices about how you use the time you're with your child, to make the most of learning opportunities as they arise. At first, such "magical moments" may seem few and far between. But with practice, you'll learn how to identify opportunities ripe with learning potential and when to let time together be just that. Once the two of you become comfortable with this shift in the way you spend time together, you'll both look forward to the experiences you share. Remember, learning is a gradual and continuous process, not an event that begins and concludes on schedule.

CHAPTER CONCEPTS

- Look for natural opportunities to share learning experiences with your child.

- Choose family activities that encourage learning.

- Make reading a family activity.

- Talk with your child.

BENEFITS & RESULTS

Child practices in real life what he learned in school.

School adds more meaning to child's everyday life.

You provide unique opportunities for child to practice skills learned in school.

CHILD IMPROVES:
- Reading skills   • Math skills
- Reasoning abilities
- Expressive language and vocabulary skills
- Problem-solving abilities
- Thought and planning skills
- Memory capabilities

Lines of communication are opened between you and your child.

You have lots of fun with your child.

Child feels like an important member of the family.

Family ties are strengthened.

You become an important factor in the growth of your child's skills.

CHAPTER 6

Building "Little Engines
Who Can"

Remember the delightful preschool story of the "little engine who can?"

At first discouraged by its small stature and limited power, the tiny locomotive knows it can never make it to the top of the mountain. The mountain is just too steep, the load too heavy. But the little engine really wants to make it to the top. *I think I can, I know I can,* he begins to chant as he chugs up the steep rails. Suddenly he's at the top, and the mountain that had been such an insurmountable obstacle is now just another hill.

■ "Little Engines" in the Classroom

So who are the "little engines who can" in the classroom? They're the kids who:

- eagerly approach new learning situations without fearing failure.

- know they are special regardless of their setbacks or accomplishments.

- engage the teacher's attention through their eagerness and determination to learn.

- credit their success to effort, not to luck or good fortune.

A strong foundation will carry kids forward and give them self-confidence and persistence.

How do you help your child become a "little engine who can?" Even though the demands of work and home may not leave you much extra time, you can use the time you have to "engineer" your child's can-do attitude.

■ Laying the Tracks

"Little engines who can" don't just happen. They develop. They need a strong foundation to carry them forward, to give them self-confidence and persistence. This foundation will help your child chug through difficult challenges. He responds to frustration by persisting and by trying harder. He is willing to explore new ideas and different approaches in his quest for answers. He can look back from the top of each mountain peak he masters and see the path of his efforts.

Fuel the Engine – Show Your Love ■

Your love for your child lays the track and fuels the engine. A child who knows you love her will see failure as an opportunity to try again. Children who know they are loved:

Your love lays the track and fuels the engine.

- will not see failure as a rejection of their self-worth.

- will have fewer behavior problems because their basic emotional needs are being met at home.

- will not be faced with emotional needs that constantly distract them from their schoolwork.

While of course *you* know you love your child, does your child know? It's easy to take for granted that she just knows you love her. Stop right now and think – when was the last time you *told* her that you love her? Children need frequent reassurance that their parents love them. Even when your busy life keeps you preoccupied, there are easy ways for you to show your love. A quick hug, a gentle touch, a warm smile, a compliment for a task well done – and the easiest of all, an "I love you." As simple as it seems, the attention you give your child's emotional needs goes a long way toward helping her become a "little engine who can."

■ Keep the Engine Running – Celebrate Your Child's Successes

When kids feel successful, they believe they can do whatever needs to be done to accomplish a task. Children succeed far more than they realize. Sometimes they just need someone to help them see their achievements. Most of us have an absolute view of progress – all or none, win or lose, have or have not. In truth, most progress results from small steps. Even the much-celebrated "overnight success" is typically many years in the making. Help your child see her small steps, and you help her stay motivated as she moves forward to bigger accomplishments.

You have many opportunities to point out your child's small steps each day. Does he play an instrument? Compliment his improvement on the passage that he's struggled to learn. Recognize his progress in reading, writing, math skills, and other abilities. Praise him for completing assignments and chores. Help him see and appreciate his progress on the way to a goal, and avoid focusing only on the goal. The child who can do so will keep putting one foot in front of the other without worrying about where the path goes, and may well end up surpassing everyone's expectations.

Add Power to the Engine –
"I Know I Can, I Know I Can" ■

School presents your child with numerous challenges that demand persistence to succeed. Long assignments, difficult material, and even redoing work to improve it are but a few of the tasks your child faces every day. Mistakes are common and frequent as she learns new skills. Building these skills requires a lot of practice, and practice isn't always fun. Neither is it pleasant to have others point out your mistakes. But these are fundamental aspects of learning. As if it's not enough that the demands of lessons grow increasingly complex, your child also must develop new strategies and approaches to overcome mistakes. It takes incredible perseverance to succeed.

Most progress results from small steps.

Look for opportunities to encourage that persistence. Praise efforts as well as outcomes. Compliment your child's work along the way as she completes a task. Notice when she is working on something that she finds particularly difficult, such as assignments that require new skills, and offer extra encouragement. Help her learn to break large tasks into small steps. A child who seems to lack persistence might well just be overwhelmed by what seems to her an enormous job. Is today's math assignment particularly long and tough? Have her do the first ten problems, then take a break. Is she frustrated to tears by the book report due next week? Have her outline what she needs to do – choose book, read book, outline main points of report, write report – and plan when she can do each.

Help your child see that his efforts make a difference. You can't do what you don't try, and your child needs to see that when he does try, he can do. Point out his progress in many areas, from athletic activities to progress in playing a musical instrument – and of course, in schoolwork.

Let your child struggle with difficult lessons and tasks. Encourage her as she struggles, but resist the natural urge to jump in to rescue her from her difficulties. Becoming involved too early interrupts the learning process, and may well make a child become dependent rather than persistent. Your child needs to learn to keep trying even when her first effort doesn't result in success. Praise her even when she doesn't succeed. "I know you didn't do as well on your spelling test as you expected. Keep trying – you'll do better next time."

The track of persistence takes time and patience to build. The earlier you start encouraging your child to keep trying, the more persistent he will become. Start looking for those small opportunities every day to emphasize the positive, no matter what your child's age.

Keep the Engine on Track –
Cultivate Responsibility ◼

Today's classrooms are busy, often crowded, places. Children compete for the teacher's attention not only with each other but with the clock as well. To do well, your child must work independently without constant supervision, follow his classroom's rules of behavior, take the initiative to complete classroom projects correctly and on time, and complete assigned homework on time. In short, your child must take responsibility for his educational experiences.

Responsibility Starts at Home

Does your child have chores? This is a good and practical way to help her develop a sense of participation and accountability. Chores give your child practice doing repetitive tasks and meeting expectations about the quality of her work – which happen to be important aspects of her school experience.

Chores not yet a part of your child's life? No problem. It's never too late to get him involved in household activities. Take a few minutes with paper and pen to list all the tasks necessary to keep everything running. Start with the daily tasks – meals, dishes, picking up around the house. Then move onto those that are essential yet less frequent – shopping, vacuuming, cleaning bathrooms, yard work, and so on. Try to

It's never too late to get your child involved in household activities.

include everything, so that you have as complete a picture as possible of what it takes to move your family through each day, week, month and year. Now, think about the age and ability of each child. Jot a family member's name beside each task. Start from where each child currently is, not from where you'd like them to be. You'll have to use your judgment about which tasks are appropriate for which kids. Depending on the size of your family and the capabilities of your children, you may find your name beside most of the tasks. Even if this is the case, make sure to involve every member of the family in some activity. It's the process of participating that matters most.

Remember that it takes time and consistency to build responsibility. Most parents know that just assigning household tasks doesn't mean that they'll get done. In fact, many parents complain that it's more work to get their kids to do their chores than to do the chores themselves! Here are some tips to move your kids toward more responsible behavior regarding chores.

- Have your child participate in the process of assigning tasks.

- Start small and with simple tasks.

- Demonstrate the right way to complete tasks.

- Rotate unpleasant tasks.

- Set clear time limits for the completion of each task.

- Provide an appropriate consequence when your child fails to complete a chore on time.

- Don't nag.

- Be consistent.

- Praise your child for the help he provides and be as specific as possible.

The best way to help your child develop responsibility is to let her experience the consequences of irresponsibility.

What do you do when your efforts fail to produce the desired results and your kids don't do their chores? Parents often moan, "We've asked him a thousand times, we've begged, we've yelled and nothing works unless we stand over him the entire time." Such situations often arise because we've thought only about what sort of consequence to provide if the child *doesn't* do the chore. Reasonable consequences are critical, but they're only part of the picture. Balance consequences with recognition and reward, simple actions like praising a job well done or letting your child stay up late to read or watch a favorite movie.

Transfer Responsibility to Schoolwork

Once you establish a pattern of responsibility around chores, it's easier to shift the same expectations and behaviors into other areas of your child's life. As crucial as the school's role is in your child's education, the responsibility for learning really lies with your child. Bringing home books, completing assignments, keeping needed supplies available, getting to class on time, and many other school activities require your child to plan, organize, and remember. This accountability is much easier for children to manage when they're already accustomed to handling responsibility.

Consequences

All that being said, it's important to let your child live with the consequences of irresponsible behavior. All too often the things we do in the interest of "helping" our children end up hindering the growth of responsibility. Do you take items to school that your child forgets? Do you make excuses for her when she fails to complete an assignment on time? As well-intended as such interventions are, they reinforce your child's irresponsible behavior. The best way to help her develop responsibility is to let her experience the consequences of her irresponsibility – kindly but firmly. Avoid taking a judgmental tone. "I'm sorry you left your science book at school. I know you must be worried about how you'll be ready for tomorrow's quiz." Often, the consequence is punishment enough. Your child may not be happy with you, and will no doubt freely express her displeasure with your choice. That's fine. Just hold your ground, and avoid getting dragged into an argument. Your child still needs your support and encouragement. What she doesn't need is for you to bail her out of a situation she created for herself.

Once your child realizes there are consequences when she fails to handle her responsiblities as she should, you will see a dramatic change in her behavior. Amazingly, she will become more responsible! She will remember her books

When your ch... feels and acts like the "little engine who can," he demonstrates self-confidence and persistence.

and papers, musical instrument, and band rehearsal. She will also become more organized and better prepared for her homework assignments. If you are not there to bail her out, she will realize that if it's going to get done, she has to do it. Even though she will become more responsible in other parts of her life, we're not promising that she'll clean her room without prodding.

■ *No Limits*

When your child feels and acts like the "little engine who can," he demonstrates self-confidence and persistence. He will blaze new tracks to reach his goals. His efforts will turn mountains into hills, and hills into speed bumps. When your "little engine" rolls, nothing stops him. He knows the value of effort, and he's not afraid to apply himself – because he also knows the joy of success.

CHAPTER CONCEPTS

- Let your child know you love him.
- Help your child become responsible.
- Build a can-do attitude.
- Recognize the importance of persistence.
- Help your child overcome mistakes.
- Keep your child motivated longer.
- Recognize the importance of chores.
- Make your child responsible for her behavior.

BENEFITS & RESULTS

YOUR CHILD:

...becomes a more responsible person.

...approaches new learning situations
without fear of failure.

...knows he is special regardless of setbacks
or accomplishments.

...engages teacher's attention by eagerness
and the determination to learn.

...credits success to effort, not to luck or good fortune.

...does not see failure as a rejection of self-worth.

...appreciates small progress, not just the goal.

...stays motivated when the going gets tough.

...becomes a more independent learner.

...takes responsibility for his own schoolwork.

...has fewer behavioral, academic and emotional problems.

...brings home books and assignments from school
without your help.

...does better on everyday schoolwork, projects and tests.

CHAPTER 7

Developing a Partnership With Your Child's School

You're a busy parent.

Most days, you scramble to get your kids off to school, well-prepared, so you can rush to work. The end of the day reverses the proccss, plus there are after-school activities and dinner and homework. When 24 hours aren't enough as it is for all that you need to do each day, where are you supposed to find time to develop a partnership with your child's school? Relax. You don't have to become a classroom volunteer or president of the parent/ teacher organization. It's easier than you think – and much more rewarding than you can imagine. This is one area where a little effort on your part goes a long, long way toward helping your child get the most from school.

> **Studies show that student grades improve when parents attend as few as two school events or activities during the school year.**

■ Why It Matters

Children are very good at reading between the lines. They can find that gap between what you say and what you do long before you even know you've created it. If you tell your child school is important, you need to show that you believe what you're saying. Studies show that student grades improve when parents attend as few as two school events or activities during the school year. Test scores, as well, are likely to go up, and discipline problems go down.

At a Minimum ■

Your time is in short supply. How do you make it count? At a minimum, attend the activities listed in the following chart.

Activity	How Often	How Long	Benefit
Parent / Teacher Conferences	Two or three times during the school year	15 to 30 minutes	Keeps you current on your child's academic and social progress.
Open House	Once or twice a year	15 to 30 minutes	Lets you see where your child spends most of his/her day, meet teachers and other school staff, and view highlights of your child's work.
Concerts and Plays	Once or twice a year	30 minutes to an hour	Showcase your child's creative abilities.

Older children still want their teachers and friends to see that you care.

Parent/teacher conferences and open houses give you a chance to meet teachers, other parents, and your child's classmates. Even if he acts like your attendance is no big deal, don't be fooled. It is. In many ways school is a home away from home for your child, who probably spends more waking hours there than at home. He wants you to see this part of his life. Younger children often want their parents to sit at their desks and look at all their books. Though older children may be outwardly less enthusiastic or even appear disinterested, they still want their teachers and friends to see that you care.

Extracurricular activities may seem like optional events to you, but to your child they're every bit as important as school (and maybe even more). This is where he has a chance to shine in front of an audience, and nothing makes that glow brighter than when you're part of the applause. Make every effort to attend.

For More Impact ∎

Your involvement in school activities other than those directly connected to your child broadens your relationship with your child's school. If your schedule permits:

- Attend at least one parent/teacher organization meeting during the school year, and more if you can squeeze the time from your calendar.

- Help with special projects for your child's class or school.

  — Serve on the "telephone team" to make contacts for special events and fund-raising activities.

  — Prepare materials for special events like art fairs, science fairs, outdoor educational activities, holiday festivities, plays, and concerts.

  — Take part in school fund-raising efforts.

- Participate on a school committee.

- Volunteer for reading time or special activities in your child's classroom.

Successful college students and young adults cite parental interest and involvement in school activities as strong motivators.

While these activities take more time, they put you in more regular contact with your child's teacher, other school staff, and other parents. They also give you more opportunity to watch and experience your child's everyday world, helping to strengthen the bond between the two of you. Does this extra involvement sound like more than your busy schedule can handle? Most parents today are in the same situation. Offer to share a volunteer task with one or more other parents. You give the school some much-needed help and perhaps draw other parents into participating. Again, an important result is that your child sees you backing your words with action by giving of a commodity more valuable than money – time.

■ *Communicating With Your Child's Teacher*

Successful college students and young adults often cite parental interest and involvement in school activities as strong motivators. Researchers believe this is a key factor in separating them from peers who are less directed in their goals and achievements. Even if your parents only went to your school for conferences and to pick you up when you were sick, their interest in your report card no doubt influenced your efforts to get good grades.

Your child's teacher is your link to school and, to an extent, to your child. She sees his everyday successes and challenges, and understands what motivates him. For his sake, establish and maintain a good relationship. Your child's teacher is far more likely to call or send a note about a small problem if you've established a clear interest in his schoolwork and progress. Who knows better than you that small problems are easier, and less time-consuming, to resolve than big ones?

When your child knows you talk with her teacher regularly, she's more likely to be honest about things that happen at school. Odds are, you'll hear about Tuesday's spelling test disaster or Thursday's hallway time-out for talking during class from her, not from another source. And you'll hear about Monday's book report "A" and Wednesday's selection as classroom helper. It's also a big boost to your child's self-esteem to see that you care. As you develop your relationship with your child's school, you strengthen your relationship with your child, too.

Introduce yourself to the teacher. Start building the common ground that will serve as a basis for future conversations.

First Contact – Open House ■

Open house is one of the "must do" events for you as a parent. This is your chance to introduce yourself to your child's teacher and to start building the common ground that will serve as the basis for

Parent/teacher conferences are checkpoints for your child's progress or problems.

future conversations. You also get to see where she spends her time. It's much easier to follow her chit-chat about daily events if you can envision in your mind's eye where she sits and where things are in the room, because she'll no doubt talk to you as if you know. Let her show you around, and ask questions. Offer positive observations about the classroom, your child's space in it, and your child's teacher. "You can see the board very well from here." and "It's nice that your teacher's desk faces the class." are the kinds of comments that show you're paying attention and that you're interested.

Usually, the teacher has some kind of presentation that provides basic information about how the classroom operates. You can expect to find out:

- the teacher's grading structure, including what assignments have special importance and what happens if work is late.

- how much homework you can expect your child to have during the week and over the weekends.

- about special projects or reports that will require extra work from your child and, possibly, assistance from you.

- what major topics the class will cover.

Do you have a special talent that your child's teacher might find useful, or an interest in helping out with classroom activities? Open house is a good opportunity to let the teacher know that even though you're busy, you want to participate.

Don't view open house as a chance to air unresolved grievances from last year or concerns you have for this year. If you need a more extensive conversation with your child's teacher before the school year gets under way, ask how to schedule an appointment for this purpose. Remember, open house is just a general introduction.

Let your child's teacher know about stressful events in your child's life.

■ Ongoing Contact – Staying in Touch

Open house gets the communication connection started. Now you need to keep it going. When you think about it, there's very little in life that provides such a great return for such a small investment of your time. Maintaining a relationship with your child's teacher throughout the school year builds trust between you and the teacher. It also demonstrates to your child that you and the teacher (or school) are allies, not adversaries.

While you don't need to see your child's teacher every day, don't wait until the first parent/teacher conference to renew your relationship. If you take your child to school every day, pop into the classroom for a quick hello every now and then. This lets you see changes in the classroom as the class moves through major topics or projects, and reinforces your interest in your child's schoolwork. It's also a great way to just ask, "How's it going?" Your child will be more likely to bring concerns to you, too, if he knows you're interested in his daily school experiences.

Notes don't have to bear bad news. Send occasional short ones to let the teacher know your child particularly enjoyed an activity or lesson. Thank the teacher for her efforts, and let her know that you see and appreciate your child's progress. Teachers enjoy hearing that they're making a positive difference in a child's life. And who knows? You could get a nice note every now and then, too!

Let your child's teacher know about stressful events in your child's life, such as health problems or the death of a family member (you don't have to give details). Your child's behavior will reflect these events, though not always in ways you might expect. The teacher will appreciate a "heads up" to help make any necessary short term accommodations to help your child get through a difficult time, or at least to understand the basis for unusual behavior.

Sometimes you'll have serious concerns about your child that need immediate attention. If grades drop off, or attitude suddenly turns sour, pick up the telephone and give the teacher a call. Many teachers make their home telephone numbers available to parents. If your child's teacher doesn't, call the school office to leave a message asking for a return call. For problems that may be bigger than ten minutes worth of conversation, schedule an appointment to meet with the teacher at a time that's convenient for you both.

■ *Parent/Teacher Conferences*

Most schools schedule parent/teacher conferences two or three times during the school year. Sometimes parents wait until the first conference to meet their child's teacher, thinking this is the reason conferences take place. Don't, because it's not! Parent/teacher conferences are checkpoints for you and the teacher to discuss your child's progress and any problems. You should expect to talk about your child's:

- Academic performance

- Social skills

- Classroom behavior

- Unique strengths and weaknesses

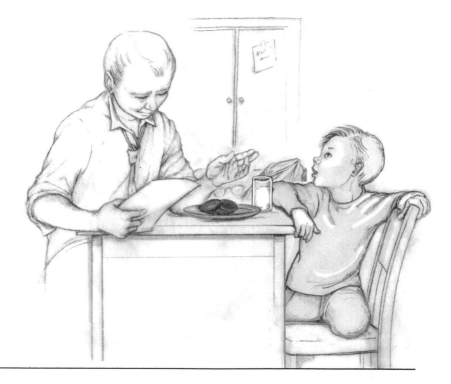

Preparing for Your Conference ■

Most parent/teacher conferences are 15 to 30 minutes long. That's not much time to cover your concerns, your child's concerns, and the teacher's concerns. Fortunately, it doesn't take much time to prepare, especially if you've already started building your relationship with your child's teacher. To get the most from parent/teacher conferences, follow these three steps.

1. Talk with your child.

Before you go for your conference, ask your child if she has any concerns she would like you to bring up with the teacher. This is a good opportunity to ask her specifically about any complaints she's shared with you recently. If a concern is important enough to your child that she wants you to talk to the teacher, there's likely an issue that you should explore a bit further. Some complaints are rooted in issues other than the obvious. Difficulty completing classroom assignments could be a sign that your child can't see the board clearly, for example, or that she becomes distracted by other activities. Discussing the concern with the teacher can help pinpoint the problem so you can work collaboratively toward a solution.

2. Prepare your questions.

Most teachers cover standard information with parents during conferences. You should leave your conference knowing the answers to these questions:

• Does my child regularly complete assignments?

• Does my child participate in classroom activities?

• How well does my child follow directions?

• Does my child make good use of independent work periods?

• Does my child get along well with adults and other students at school?

• Does my child need additional help in any academic area?

• Is there anything I can do at home to help my child's progress?

If your child has problems, ask the teacher for suggestions that will help you, your child, and the teacher work together to resolve them. (See chapter 8 for more on homework problems and chapter 11 for more on other problems.)

3. Be prepared to listen.

The teacher may also have concerns to discuss with you. Stay focused on the issues, and keep your child's interests foremost. If you have a good relationship with your child's teacher and have been in regular communication throughout the school year, your conference should yield few surprises. If you disagree with the teacher's comments, wait until he's finished presenting them before you respond. Take a moment to think through your questions and responses. Keep your tone pleasant and agreeable. If you cannot do so – perhaps the comments catch you off guard, or are completely at odds with what you were expecting – you and the teacher both might be better served if you simply say you'd like to think about the teacher's comments and schedule another appointment to discuss them. This gives both of you some distance, and also gives you a chance to talk with your child if you need to get her perspective.

If you have been in regular communication throughout the school year, your conference should yield few surprises.

Let your child know, at least in general terms, how the conference went. Children are curious about what their teachers have to say about them. Be sure to share any compliments the teacher offered (most teachers try to say something positive no matter what kind of problems there are). This is particularly important if your child has shown progress in areas of struggle. Did the teacher identify areas that need improvement? Discuss the steps you, your child, and the teacher will take to help those improvements happen. Keep a positive tone, even when talking about problems.

Did the teacher's comments come as a surprise? Were there things about your child's school performance and behavior that you didn't know about before the conference? If so, your relationship with your child's school still needs improvement. Don't let yourself get caught unaware again. Starting now, use the suggestions in this chapter to begin building a relationship that keeps you connected to your child's school life.

CHAPTER CONCEPTS

- Attend <u>at least</u> 2 school functions:
  Open House & conference are a must.

- Offer to help with some class activity,
  something you can do at home.

- Send occasional short positive notes to the teacher.

- Be prepared for Parent / Teacher conferences.

- If you drive kids to school, occasionally pop in
  and say hi to the teacher.

BENEFITS & RESULTS

Test scores increase.

Discipline problems decrease.

Teacher is more likely to keep you informed.

Child realizes that you and the teacher are allies.

Talking about school is more comfortable
between you and your child.

Problems are easier to work through with the teacher.

Child tries harder in class.

Trust builds between you and the teacher.

CHAPTER 8

Homework

It's been a long day,
and what you really want to do
is crash on the couch.

Instead, you're answering telephone sales pitches, feeding the cat, putting in a load of laundry, and fixing dinner. "I don't get this," whines your child, who is working on her homework at the kitchen table. "I need help!" The best way to handle this demand is to...

____ Stop what you're doing, sit down with her, and help her through the assignment that's giving her trouble.

____ Tell her to move on to the next problem, you're busy and tired right now and will help her later.

____ Throw your hands up in the air, scream that no one cares about how *your* day went, and stomp out of the room.

Choosing the last option is tempting, isn't it? The other two choices aren't much better, though. The truth is, there really is no easy answer to this common predicament. Homework hassles are among the most common sources of tension and difficulty between working parents and their children. For as long as your child is in school, these struggles will be part of your life. Take heart – there are simple steps you can take to minimize these hassles and at the same time help him get the most out of his homework assignments.

Mastery comes only through time and repetition.

■ Why Homework, Anyway?

So what is it with homework, anyway? Your child already spends most of his waking hours in a classroom. Why doesn't he learn what he needs to learn there, where the teacher can help him work through lessons he doesn't understand? After all, isn't that why he goes to school in the first place? Life would be so much easier for him and for you if he just did all his schoolwork at school!

Nothing worthwhile comes without effort, and learning is no exception. Academic skills like reading, math, and writing require much practice to master. That mastery comes only through time (years, not hours and days) and repetition. As difficult as it makes your life when you catch the fallout of your child's frustration, the only way she will learn (and master) such skills is by doing them over and over and over, on her own.

Homework helps kids become independent learners. Homework forces your child to work on assignments without someone providing direction for every step. This encourages him to accept accountability for doing his work correctly and accurately. He, not his teacher, monitors homework assignments.

Homework also teaches your child self-management and organization. Homework demands that your child use a variety of organizational skills. Many assignments require her to find appropriate resources, collect needed materials, budget her time, and meet deadlines. These are all skills that not only help her to complete her homework assignments, but ones that also will serve her well in her adult life.

Most children do best when they can work in an area set aside for homework and study.

Where to Do Homework ■

Where is the best place for your child to do homework? The short answer is anywhere he can work comfortably and without distraction. Most, though not all, children do best when they can work in an area set aside for homework and study. A designated study area gives your child a place to keep his learning tools all in the same place. Being in this area evokes a sense of purpose within your child, and helps him focus on the tasks at hand. This study area need not be fancy or extensive. A desk or table to provide a flat writing surface, located in a corner of your child's bedroom or a room in your house that is removed from the general flow of traffic, meets typical study needs. A bookshelf provides a place to keep her paper, pens and pencils, notebooks, textbooks, and reference items. A desk lamp or other adjustable light source assures adequate lighting.

A good number of children prefer a more casual, relaxed atmosphere for homework and study. Some like to settle in on the couch or the floor, books spread out around them. Others like to sit at the kitchen table, within easy reach of a snack and perhaps some help from mom or dad. This is fine, as long as there are few distractions to draw your child's attention away from homework. Again, your child needs a flat surface for writing, some space to organize books and materials, adequate lighting, and minimal distractions. Often, as children grow older they migrate to study locations where they can close themselves off from the rest of the household, particularly when studying for tests.

Your child needs a flat surface, space to organize materials, adequate lighting, and minimal distractions.

One "no" rule: no television! **Do not let your child do his homework with the television on.** No matter how hard he tries, he cannot ignore what's happening on TV. Television is simply too distracting. It is important for your child to learn how to study, and to do so in an environment that supports good study habits. Doing homework in front of the TV reinforces bad study habits.

How Much Homework to Expect ■

Homework amounts vary greatly from school to school and sometimes from teacher to teacher. In general, elementary school children typically have about 10 minutes of homework for every grade level. For example, your first grader would have 10 minutes of homework, while your fifth grader might have 50 minutes worth of assignments.

Find out at the beginning of the school year what to expect for your child. In elementary school, teachers usually address the topic of homework at open house. If your child's teacher doesn't, feel free to bring it up or to send a note asking how much homework to expect.

It's harder to predict homework levels when your child reaches middle school and high school, since she has more than one teacher. You can often get a sense of how much homework to expect at orientation or open house. You can also check with each teacher by note or by telephone. Knowing how much homework your child is likely to have helps you plan study time.

Children typically have about 10 minutes of homework for every grade level.

■ *When to Do Homework*

Your child should make homework and study a routine part of every day. Start this practice when your child first enters school. Set aside a regular, scheduled study time for your child to do her homework assignments. Younger children who may not have homework every day should still have daily study time. They can use this time for related activities that help them practice academic skills, such as reading or writing. Encourage older children (middle school and high school) who don't have assigned homework on a particular day to use study time for similar activities. When you know your child does her homework regularly and does well in school, you might allow her to use study time as she sees fit.

No one time for doing homework works for all children. Some kids are still charged and ready to keep learning when they come home from school. Others are tired and need to unwind. What is most important is that you establish a scheduled time each day for doing homework and studying. Involve your child in deciding when this time will be. If she has no homework and doesn't need to prepare for a test, she can use the time to read. Be sure study time fits in with the activity patterns of your household. Consider your schedule as well as family commitments or the schedules of other children. If your child's choice is practical, go with it. This increases the likelihood that she will use the scheduled time with minimal fuss. If you have more than one child, try to schedule study periods for the same time. This keeps children from distracting each other, and cuts down on the level of supervision you need to provide.

Establish a scheduled time each day for doing homework and studying.

Encourage your child to finish homework 30 to 45 minutes before bedtime, so he has some free time and can relax before going to bed. This helps keep homework from interfering with bedtime routines. You may find this difficult at first, especially if your child is older when you implement study periods. With persistence and support, he will adapt – and will develop better time-management skills in the process.

In the end, the study procedures you establish benefit both you and your child. Your child develops good study habits, and gets her assignments done and in on time. You have fewer hassles over homework, and may even get some time for yourself while your child studies.

■ *How Much Help Should I Give My Child?*

Many parents have a difficult time deciding just how much help with homework assignments to give their children. It's easy to focus on the goal of just getting the assignment done, overlooking long term goals like developing independent study habits. In general, it is your child's responsibility to:

- know what his assignments are, and when they are due.

- have all the materials he needs to complete his assignments (books, paper, pens and pencils, reference materials, other resources).

- do his assignments with minimal or no assistance.

- turn his completed assignments in on time.

Parents often get caught in the trap of assuming far more responsibility for homework than they should. This is a natural aspect of your concern for your child's progress in school. After all, you want your child to succeed, and you accept that you have a role in helping that happen. But remember that your role is to support, not lead. If you continually step in to carry your child through homework assignments that challenge him, your concern can end up sabotaging his long term success. Those struggles to understand academic concepts are often a vital part of the learning process.

When young children first begin bringing assignments home, it's both reasonable and important to give them plenty of encouragement. You might need to sit nearby while your child does her homework, so she feels your presence and support. She might need your help with certain parts of her assignment, or even your participation (such as listening to her read aloud or practicing her spelling words). But remember that this is your child's homework, not yours. She won't learn if you do it for her.

Is it OK to answer your child's questions? Of course. It's even OK to help solve a problem or two, or to explain a simple point your child doesn't quite understand. Just don't let yourself become a homework assistant – stick strictly to the role of advisor.

Your child's struggles to understand are a vital part of the learning process.

- **Look for the positive and avoid criticism.** Your child's frustration will only increase if he's having a rough time and you continue to point out his shortcomings. Statements like "You should be able to do these on your own by now!" or "Haven't we been over this enough?" can quickly turn a homework session into a war zone. Most kids would rather fight with a parent than continue struggling with their homework.

- **Beware the "That's not the way my teacher does it" trap.** This familiar song deserves a polite refrain from you in response – "Sorry, dear, it looks like I'm not going to be very helpful, then." Arguing about how to do an assignment seldom produces completed homework, though it does result in an entertaining distraction. Suggest that your child mark the problem or assignment for discussion with her teacher, and move on to the next assignment. Learning to ask for help when you are confused or don't understand is an important skill.

- **Checking homework is OK, but leave it at that.** Checking your child's homework is a simple way to show that you're interested in how things are going. It can also draw you into an argument. "This looks pretty good, but I don't think the answers to the last four problems are correct," you offer, intending to be helpful. Your child is likely to respond with an indignant rebuttal that she's worked *really* hard, she'll *never* get it right, and wind up with a mournful finale, "I guess I'll just *fail* math." Save yourself the melodrama. Check her work for completeness, not correctness.

For more information about how to be effective in helping your child with schoolwork, see Chapter 9, *So You Want to Help Your Child With Schoolwork*.

Your child should be able to complete assignments independently.

Coping with Chronic Homework Problems ■

When your child consistently fails to complete homework assignments, you need to step in. Can your child usually complete his assignments with extra assistance and encouragement? On most evenings, he should be able to complete his assignments independently. If he seems to require more help from you than you think is reasonable, it's time to schedule an appointment with your child's teacher.

Explain your concerns to the teacher. Ask if your child is able to complete similar assignments in class. Does the teacher think your child has the skills to do the work? If not, there's more information for you in Chapter 11, *When Your Child Has Problems*. If the teacher believes your child is capable of doing his work and does fine

*Set up a plan
with the teacher
to get your child
back on track.*

in class, you need to set up a plan with the teacher to get your child back on track with his homework.

■ *A Plan for Improvement*

While your child's specific plan for improvement must accommodate her unique circumstances, there are several key principles to follow in setting up that plan.

- • *Your child's homework is her responsibility.* Your child needs to know what her assignments are, when they are due, and how much time she should plan to complete them.

- • *Establish clear expectations.* What do you and the teacher expect your child to do? Make these expectations clear to your child, and make sure he understands that you and the teacher are working together to define them. Often a meeting involving you, your child, and the teacher is the best setting to establish expectations.

- • *Establish clear consequences.* Determine what will happen if your child fails to meet the expectations you and the teacher have established, and let your child know what consequences to expect. Identify several activities or privileges your child enjoys every day. When he meets the established expectations, he continues to enjoy his activities or privileges. When he doesn't, some or all may be suspended. When you must suspend privileges, do so matter-of-factly, without anger or emotion. Be consistent.

- **Stay connected with your child's teacher.** A simple "note home" system is an easy and effective way to know whether your child is meeting established expectations. Your child's teacher just sends home a short note each day telling you whether your child has completed and turned in her assignments. Your child's failure to bring her daily note home means you automatically assume she did not do or turn in her assignments, and implement the appropriate consequences.

■ *It's Never Too Late to Start*

The earlier in your child's school years that you can implement effective home-work practices, the more likely you are to shape homework as a positive learning experience. But it's never too late to start. Even if your child has reached the grumbling and complaining stage, you can still turn things around. Sit down with him, at a time and in a place where there are no distractions, and explain what you plan to do and what you expect to accomplish. Involve him in your plans as much as possible. Does he have a favorite place or time to study? When practical and consistent with other suggestions in this chapter, incorporate his preferences into your approach.

In reality, your child doesn't like fighting about homework any more than you do. Though you may hear complaints and even encounter resistance at first, stick to your plan. Remember, stay calm and keep it positive. In the end, both you and your child will appreciate having homework as just another routine in the day.

CHAPTER CONCEPTS

- Why kids get homework.

- Setting up a homework space.

- How much homework should the child expect?

- When is the best time to do homework?

- How much help should you give your child?

- How should you help your child?

- How to deal with chronic homework problems.

BENEFITS & RESULTS

YOUR CHILD:

...learns to make homework a routine.

...improves test scores.

...assumes accountability for her homework.

...earns better grades.

...becomes a more independent learner.

...improves retention of skills taught in the classroom.

...becomes more responsible.

...develops self-management skills.

PLUS:

Homework interferes less with bedtime routines.

Homework is completed with far fewer hassles.

Chronic homework problems are eliminated.

WORKING PARENTS CAN RAISE SMART KIDS

CHAPTER 9

So You Want to Help Your Child With Schoolwork

You're a responsive, caring parent.

You watch your child grapple with her schoolwork, and you want to help. After all, you want her to succeed in school, to do the best that she can. You want to make school easier and more enjoyable. Before you grab a pencil and pull up a chair, take heed! Your help might make a difference for your child... but not in the ways you intended.

■ When Not to Help

For the most part, your child gets the most from his educational experiences when he experiences them himself. Trial and error is a normal part of the learning process, even if it's sometimes slow and frustrating. As tempting as it is to step in and speed your child past his frustrations, resist. Before leaving the sideline, ask yourself these three questions:

- Is my child asking for my assistance? If not, and there are no apparent problems at school (your child's grades are acceptable and the teacher is satisfied with your child's performance), stay on the sideline.

- Does my child do homework on time and get satisfactory grades? If so, stay on the sideline.

- Is my child's teacher concerned about my child's academic performance? If not, stay on the sideline.

It's OK for your child to do "fine" in school. While of course you want him to do his best, he doesn't have to get A's on all his assignments. If his schoolwork meets the teacher's expectations, he's doing "fine," and that should be fine with you. It's easy to put too much pressure on your child to do better, which can have the opposite, undesired effect of undermining his well-being and attitude toward learning.

Helper, Beware! ■

Even when your child needs or wants your help with schoolwork, your involvement can deteriorate to tears and arguments before you realize what's happening. Tension-filled help sessions do little to improve your child's learning and can do significant harm to your relationship with your child.

It's frustrating to be unable to transfer your knowledge to your child.

You embark on your help session with the best of intentions. But there are more bumps than you expect. Suddenly, your child starts crying. What's going through her mind? *You think I'm stupid! I don't understand. That's not what my teacher showed us in class. All you do is yell at me! Why can't I get this?* It's hard for your child to face the reality that she can't do her schoolwork, and to admit this to you.

A parent's thoughts are similar. *Why doesn't he get this? It's so simple! Are all the other kids having so much trouble with this? I don't understand why the teacher can't teach this in a way that makes sense to my child. Maybe I haven't been paying as much attention as I should – I should've picked up on this problem long ago. He's never going to succeed in school, or in life, for that matter. If he fails, what does that say about me as a parent?* It's frustrating to be unable to transfer your knowledge to your child.

■ *Keeping Tensions in Check*

Kids and parents alike bring a lot of "baggage" to schoolwork help sessions. Your child wants to do well and make you proud. You want to show her how to do well. Somehow, though, you often end up angry and frustrated with each other. Fortunately, there are ways to start your help sessions out on the right track... and keep them there.

Help Session Checklist ■

Is this a good time to help your child with schoolwork? Run through this quick checklist before getting started.

Am I hungry?	Yes ___	No ___
Is my child hungry?	Yes ___	No ___
Am I tired?	Yes ___	No ___
Is my child tired?	Yes ___	No ___
Did I have a bad day at work?	Yes ___	No ___
Is my child upset for any reason?	Yes ___	No ___
Is it near bedtime?	Yes ___	No ___
Is there something else I need to do?	Yes ___	No ___
Am I ready to do this work for my child if he or she can't do it?	Yes ___	No ___

If you answer "yes" to any of these questions, now is probably not the best time to help with schoolwork. If you decide to go ahead anyway, proceed with great caution. Either of you might be more on edge than usual.

Mistakes are a necessary part of the learning process.

■ What Teachers Know That Parents Don't Remember

Teachers sometimes seem to have the patience of saints. They explain and explain and explain again. Teachers know what parents have forgotten: mistakes and setbacks are a necessary part of the learning process. They don't mean that your child will fail in life. Everybody makes mistakes, and your child is no exception.

■ Teaching Like a Teacher

One disadvantage parents face when trying to help their own children with schoolwork is that they're too close. As a parent, you have a deep interest in your child's success. This makes it difficult for you to maintain objectivity... and easy for you to lose your cool when the going gets tough. What if, during your help sessions, you could view your child as, say, the neighbor's kid or one of your child's friends? After all, it's easier to keep your distance (and your cool) when you're helping someone else's child. Shifting perspective in this way helps you take a kinder, gentler approach when your child says, "I don't get it."

Helping with Specific Problems ■

When you're helping your child with a specific problem, ask him to show you what he doesn't understand. Be patient, and give him enough time to give you a full explanation. Have him start through the problem, step-by-step. Ask him to explain what he's doing, and why, at each step. This shows you what he's thinking as he's working through the problem. Often, just going through the work in this step-by-step manner causes your child to work more carefully and come up with the solution on his own. If this happens, ask him to tell you what he had been doing wrong, and what he did to correct his approach.

Sometimes the solution still eludes your child. Try creating a similar problem for her to work on instead. This helps her focus on the process of solving the problem rather than on the assignment to do the problem. Work through this created problem step-by-step, explaining each action you take. Then create a second problem, and have your child work through it. Stop at each step and have her explain it. Next, have her go back and do the original problem. Check her work, then create one last problem to be sure she understands.

If, after several attempts, your child still doesn't understand, circle the original problem on the assignment paper (or write it on another sheet of paper). Write a brief note to the teacher asking him to help your child learn how to do the problem. Should you just give your child the answer if she

> *Have your child start through the problem, step-by-step.*

can't get to it herself? With rare exceptions, no. You already know how to do the problem, so you don't learn anything. And your child still *doesn't* know how to do the problem, so she hasn't learned anything, either.

Offer to show your child the way you would solve the problem.

■ "That's Not How My Teacher Does It"

While there are often several ways to solve a math problem or write a paragraph, your child wants to do these tasks the same way the teacher does them. You may have learned different approaches, either in school or through your work experiences. Ask your child to explain how his teacher does the assigned work. If the explanation makes sense to you, switch to the teacher's approach. Sometimes your child can't explain the teacher's way because he doesn't understand it. When this is the case, there isn't much you can do. Explain, calmly, that you can't do it the teacher's way. Offer to show your child the way you would solve the problem. If he declines, ask him to have the teacher show him the process again, or write a note to the teacher describing where your child seems to be stuck.

■ Helping with Projects

Projects often involve skills that require additional instruction and practice outside the classroom, such as organizational skills, time management, and long-term planning.

In helping with projects, your role is one of guidance and direction rather than intervention or direct assistance.

Make sure your child knows exactly what the project requirements are and has planned a timetable to get the project finished. He should know when he needs to start working on the project and roughly how long each part of the project will take. Help him establish a production plan that includes a list of the materials and resources he needs to complete the project. Review progress at each stage of the project, so both you and your child know whether any information is missing. He should complete the project before its due date to allow time for final revisions.

Don't help your child with any production or construction for the project. This is her project, and should represent her best efforts – not yours. While the end result might not be as polished as it would be if you helped out, your child will learn more, and feel more pride about, doing it herself.

Your child's project should represent her best efforts – not yours.

■ *Golden Rules for Helping Your Child*

One advantage of working with your child as though he's the neighbor kid is that it's easier for you to keep your frustrations in check. When your frustrations spill over, your child feels hopeless and stupid. It's essential for you to prevent this, for your sake and for your child's well-being. *Always* be encouraging. "This is hard for everyone." "Don't worry, we'll find a way that makes sense to you." "You almost got it that time, so let's go back and see where you slipped off track." Your words can work wonders for your child's self-confidence and ability to do his schoolwork. They also help keep you calm and focused on solutions rather than the child's struggles. Be patient, and give your child all the time he needs to work through the problem.

CHAPTER CONCEPTS

- When *not* to help your child.
- Helper beware.
- Help session checklist.
- What teachers know that parents forget.
- Helping with specific problems.
- Dealing with "That's not the way my teacher did it."
- Golden rules for helping your child.
- How to help with projects.

BENEFITS & RESULTS

YOUR CHILD:

...develops organizational, time management, planning skills.

...becomes a more independent learner.

...improves self-confidence to attack difficult problems.

PLUS:

Parent and child anxieties are reduced.

Hassles are minimized.

You know the best times to help – and when *not* to help.

You are more accomplished during help sessions.

You reduce your child's frustrations with schoolwork.

You think more like a teacher.

You learn to take mistakes in stride.

You improve your working relationship with your child.

You know how to help your child find solutions to problems.

CHAPTER 10

Learning and Television

Television:
miracle of technology or the
greatest "brain drain" ever created?

Little garners more attention in this era of electronics than discussion about how much television is too much for children. Two hours a day? Four hours? What about weekends? Which programs are good for children and which ones are not? Can watching television be a family activity, or is it a waste of valuable time? For many parents, there are far more questions than answers.

That is often the case for child development experts as well. Some warn that any time in front of the tube damages a child's emerging social and academic skills. Others look at measures of those skills – behavior, grades, attitudes – and offer age-based recommendations that permit moderate viewing. While studies of how television-viewing habits affect child development seldom produce consistent results, they do show that today's children log an astonishing number of hours in front of the TV.

■ How Much Time Children Watch Television – American Academy of Pediatrics

Age Group	Average Hours Per Week Watching Television
Preschool (ages 1 to 4)	28
Elementary and junior high (ages 5 to 14)	25
High school (ages 15 to 18)	28

There are many reasons to find these numbers alarming. Critics charge that the majority of today's television programming is inappropriate for children. Content typically presents cultural stereotyping, misinformation about sexuality and human relationships, and the use of violence to resolve problems. But content isn't the entire issue. There is programming worth watching, and there are ways parents can use television as a learning tool. There isn't anything worth watching *this much*, however. The main concern is that when kids are watching television, there are many other things they aren't doing – homework, reading, physical activity, games, and even play – that require active involvement.

Kids watching television are not doing things that require active involvement.

Is it really possible to cut down on the amount of time that kids spend in front of the TV? After all, the television is such a mainstay of the modern home environment that many families have several sets in different locations around the house. The key is really moderation; too much of anything can be destructive. It may take some time and planning to change your family's television viewing habits in a way that will be more productive for your child's learning. Once you've established a family viewing program, however, you'll find the effort well worth it.

This chapter offers general suggestions to help you evaluate and possibly change your family's viewing habits. The bibliography provides recommendations for further reading for those who would like more information about television and children.

*The average
TV viewing time
for most families
is far too much.*

■ *How Much Is Too Much?*

So how much television is OK? Most educators, pediatricians and child development specialists agree that four hours a day – the average viewing time for most families – is far too much. It's difficult to establish an exact limit, however. Some authors suggest that the best strategy is simply to eliminate television viewing altogether. This is not usually a realistic strategy for most families. Instead, try limiting a child's viewing to 1 to 2 hours a day (including when you're not home). This cuts viewing time almost in half for many families. This seems a more reasonable goal than eliminating all television.

Just how much time does your family presently spend watching television? Keep a simple TV viewing log for several weeks to get a picture of what's happening in your home. This needn't be a complicated process, and it can show you how much TV time you need to cut out to reach a goal of two or fewer hours of television viewing a day.

Try to keep a realistic perspective on how much time you actually have available as you decide how much of it you want to spend watching television. For example, if your family gets home at six in the evening, spends an hour to two hours fixing and eating dinner, and your child has an hour's worth of homework or more, you don't have two hours of time for television!

Make TV Limits – and Viewing –
a Process of Family Participation ■

Your efforts are far more likely to succeed if you approach limiting TV time as a family project. Kids pay far more attention to what you do than to what you say. If your favorite indulgence is to kick back in front of the television while lecturing your child on the importance of reading, which message do you think she picks up?

Many households have the television turned on whether or not anyone is watching. Turn it off! Watch TV as a conscious choice, not just because you decided to sit in a certain chair and there was a television on in front of it. Have your child ask before they turn on the television. This helps him develop an awareness of his viewing habits.

Be wary of programs that perpetuate stereotypes and messages that conflict with your family's values.

After you determine how much time your family should spend watching television, establish a viewing schedule. Gather family members together for a few minutes each week to decide how to best use the available viewing time. Identify programs that you will watch with your child as well as those your child can watch on her own. Include shows that are educational in nature, and be wary of those that perpetuate stereotypes and messages that conflict with your family's values.

Plan other activities to fill the time you previously spent watching television. There are literally hundreds of things you can do instead of watching television that are more interactive and offer opportunities to use learning skills, from playing board games to going places.

WORKING PARENTS CAN RAISE SMART KIDS

Make TV Viewing Interactive ■ No rating system replaces your good judgment.

One of the biggest problems with television is that watching it is a passive activity. You simply sit in front of it, and it entertains you. You don't have to talk back, think, or even look like you're paying attention. Yet your consciousness is so fully captured that you literally "tune out" other events and distractions. This passive engagement is what most concerns child development experts. At best, too much TV wastes time. At worst, those tube-time behaviors transfer to other settings and activities in what becomes a counterproductive "don't-have-to-do" attitude.

You can change this. Many shows and videos can serve as a springboard for conversations with your child. Talking to kids about what they watch on TV can help them improve reasoning skills, build bigger vocabularies, and become more critical consumers. They might even become more selective viewers! Often just answering questions and sharing views can be both informative and interesting.

The television rating system, officially known as the *TV Parental Guidelines*, can help your family choose programs appropriate for your child's age. The guidelines apply to all television programming except news, sports, and unedited movies shown on premium cable channels. Under this rating system, a TV program designated as "TV-Y," for example, is appropriate for young children to watch.

One designated as "TV-MA," on the other hand, is intended for adult audiences and is considered inappropriate for children under age 17. While these designations are a good starting point for you to choose suitable television programs for your children to watch, remember that no rating system replaces your good judgment.

■ *A Little Help from Technology*

As every parent knows, agreeing to guidelines and limits doesn't mean children will follow them. When a parent isn't home, it's just too tempting for a child to do a little channel surfing. Unfortunately, many programs that are intended for adult viewing can be just a click away from your child.

When your family watches and discusses programs together, television becomes a productive, interactive activity.

The same technology that has made program choices nearly endless through satellite and premium cable services also offers a solution for concerned parents – the V-chip. Similar to the technology that enables a television to decode closed-captioning signals, the V-chip decodes rating information. Federal law requires television sets manufactured after 1996 to include V-chips. Parents can program a television's V-chip to block certain ratings, preventing the TV from receiving the show's signal.

A Little TV Goes a Long Way ■

When your family watches and discusses
programs together, moderate television
viewing becomes a productive, interactive
activity. Choosing what and when to watch
can help make the television in your home
a constructive tool that contributes to
your child's success rather than simply
gobbling up large amounts of free time.

It is important to limit TV time to encourage and sometimes push children to entertain themselves. Your child, particularly if already an avid viewer, will likely protest – loudly and often – that this limitation is unfair and life without television is unbearably boring. Amazingly, as soon as he realizes that these protests are ineffective, he finds many other activities with which to occupy himself. You may even find your child *voluntarily* choosing to do something else instead of watching TV after a while!

CHAPTER CONCEPTS

- The problem with too much TV.

- How much is too much?

- Setting up a viewing schedule.

- Setting limits.

- Making TV viewing interactive – a chance for learning.

- Making TV a family activity.

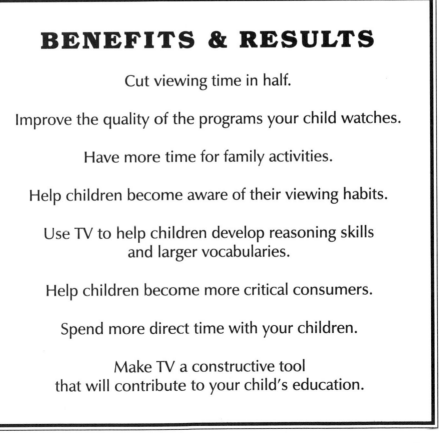

BENEFITS & RESULTS

Cut viewing time in half.

Improve the quality of the programs your child watches.

Have more time for family activities.

Help children become aware of their viewing habits.

Use TV to help children develop reasoning skills
and larger vocabularies.

Help children become more critical consumers.

Spend more direct time with your children.

Make TV a constructive tool
that will contribute to your child's education.

CHAPTER 11

When Your Child Has Problems

Most kids have problems at some time during their school years.

Fortunately, most are short-lived – struggles with fractions, resistance over homework, challenges with grammar. For the most part, tending to the small troubles in your child's life keeps them from becoming major problems. Daily conversation about schoolwork and school events keeps the lines of communication open, giving you and your child the opportunity to discuss the challenges she experiences. When your child has a generally positive attitude toward school and feels comfortable talking with you about school, you're in a good position to detect problems as they begin to develop, and your child knows you'll work with her to resolve her difficulties.

■ *When Is a Problem Serious?*

When difficulties become the rule rather than the exception, it's time for you to intervene.

So how do you know when a problem is serious and when you should get involved? Sometimes, you learn that your child is having problems in school only when the school contacts you. In most situations, however, there are early signs of trouble that can tip you off ...if you know what to look for and what questions to ask.

Minor Problems

Conflicts with peers and teachers. Problems with tests. Every child has a few bad times. As long as your child's "down" periods are infrequent and brief, let him work through them on his own. Children who are independent learners and who have positive attitudes about themselves and about school can, and should, resolve minor difficulties with little intervention from their parents. This teaches your child problem-solving skills that will serve him well throughout his life.

When your child faces minor problems, give her a sympathetic ear, but don't offer suggestions or solutions unless she asks (and even then with caution). Often, just talking through the problem leads to its resolution. If your child asks for your assistance, help her come up with her own solutions rather than telling her what to do. For example, you might ask:

- What have you already tried to solve this problem?

- What else do you think you could try?

Major Problems

In most cases, it's the number of times (or length of time) a particular problem occurs that pushes it over the line from minor to major. When peer and teacher conflicts, poor grades, school discipline, and homework difficulties become the rule rather than the exception, it's time for you to intervene. Severe behaviors such as fighting, stealing or confronting an adult at school will require your immediate attention. And when your child's school contacts you, get involved! Most schools are too busy to contact parents for minor problems.

Setting the Stage for Intervention

Confronting a problem your child is having can be a difficult experience for you as a parent. It's natural to blame yourself or the school, and to look for quick solutions to what may be difficult problems. It's hard to hear feedback about your child that isn't particularly positive. And it's easy to interpret such feedback as a criticism of your parenting skills. But laying blame, even accurately, seldom encourages good solutions. Resist the natural tendency to shut down and become defensive. Listen closely, and gather as much information about the problem as possible before responding.

Generally, problems that require your intervention fall into two basic categories, academic and social.

■ *Academic Problems*

At the risk of sounding like a broken record, we have to say this again: prevention is the best form of intervention. Major problems don't sprout overnight. They grow over weeks and months, the combined result of many little difficulties. This is not to say that you can prevent all academic problems. What you can do is intervene before your child becomes disheartened and his behavior becomes an issue.

Warning Signs

Kids often send signals that all is not well in the classroom. Admittedly, sometimes these signals are weak and ambiguous, and easier to identify in hindsight. How many of the following statements are true for your child? Put a check in front of all that apply.

☐ Avoids bringing home or sharing samples of schoolwork.

☐ Reluctant to talk about school activities.

☐ Does not complete or turn in assignments.

☐ Becomes frustrated or emotional when doing homework.

☐ Frequently makes negative comments about own academic abilities.

☐ Frequently makes negative comments about school or teachers.

☐ Gets poor grades on tests or assignments.

Both you and the teacher share a common interest in your child's success.

If any of these statements describe your child, it's time for you to step in. Start by scheduling an appointment with the teacher to discuss your observations. Approach the dialogue from a win-win perspective. Remember, both you and the teacher share a common interest in your child's success. Expect this discussion to address two primary issues:

- Is my child struggling because he *can't* do the work, or because he *won't* do the work?

- How can I work with the school and my child to resolve the problems?

Can't or Won't?

Sometimes, a child simply *won't* do schoolwork. Despite your efforts to help your child appreciate the importance of getting a good education, his behavior doesn't reflect this value. Often, the solution is simple. Tell your child, calmly and directly, that his behavior is unacceptable. A surprising number of kids respond with positive improvement to such a straightforward message. If the behavior continues after such a warning, it's time to implement a simple system such as that described in Chapter 8, *Homework*, that connects completed responsibilities with privileges. Kids are remarkably responsive when privileges that they have come to take for granted become contingent upon getting their schoolwork done.

What if you suspect your child *can't* do her schoolwork? Again, the earlier you identify learning difficulties, the more effectively you can work with your child and her teacher to resolve them. First, discuss your concerns with the teacher. Describe specific examples of your child's schoolwork that concern you. The teacher sees your child's work every day, and knows how it compares with the work of other students.

If the teacher feels there is nothing for you to worry about, then stop worrying! Some learning just takes time and practice. If the teacher agrees that your child has a problem, or contacts you first, it's time to develop a plan to get your child the additional help she needs. Again, remember that you and the teacher are partners in this plan, not adversaries. You both want your child to do her best. Be sure the action plan includes a clear understanding of responsibilities and expectations. Who is to do what, and with what goals in mind? You'll need clear, open, and regular communication to establish, implement, and evaluate a plan of action to help your child.

If the teacher asks you to work with your child at home, be sure you clearly understand what the teacher expects you to do. Chapter 9, *So You Want to Help Your Child with Schoolwork*, offers additional suggestions.

The earlier you identify learning difficulties, the more effectively you can work with your child and her teacher to resolve them.

*A tutor
may help
your child
catch up,
regain confidence,
and get back
on track.*

Getting Additional Assistance

Your child's teacher is your first resource for locating additional, appropriate assistance for your child. Typical options include:

- A peer tutor program, where older children with strong skills in key academic areas work with younger children. Such tutoring often takes place during recess or right after school, and is available at no cost to parents.

- Parent volunteers who work with children to improve skills in reading, language comprehension, math, science, and other areas. These services usually take place during regular school hours and are available at no cost.

In addition to resources available through your child's school, you might decide to seek additional assistance from outside resources. Most communities offer numerous organizations and individuals that provide private tutoring for students who are having difficulty. A tutor can often help your child catch up, regain confidence, and get back on track. Exhaust the possibilities the school offers before you select outside resources, and then discuss your plans with your child's teacher. It's especially important that outside assistance relates to the work your child is doing in school.

When Academic Problems Continue

Sometimes your child's problems persist despite your efforts to resolve them. You or the school can request an evaluation to determine if your child needs and is eligible for special education services. Many parents want to have such an evaluation conducted outside the school system to obtain a more "objective" result. This raises the important issue of trust – if you can't trust your child's school to conduct such an evaluation, how can you trust it to educate your child? In general, it's most effective to allow the school to conduct an evaluation first. Then if you find yourself at odds with the results, you can always obtain a second opinion from a specialist outside the school system. Clinical psychologists with a background in educational assessment typically conduct these evaluations.

Social adjustment and classroom behavior are significant aspects of the learning experience.

When a child needs special assistance, it becomes even more important for parents to work aggressively to build and maintain positive attitudes toward school and learning. All children have areas in which they are more competent than others. Keep your whole child in view, and celebrate your child's strengths.

■ Social and Behavior Problems

In some ways, school would be much easier if learning was simply a matter of academics. But it's not. Social adjustment and classroom behavior are significant aspects of the learning experience, and are important for your child's success both in school and later in life.

The Importance of Friends

Some children have a small number of very close friends, while others may have large networks of friends. Some friendships last for years, while others come and go like fashion fads. There are many variations in the kinds of friends children have, and your child's friendship patterns may change over time. What matters most is that your child can make and keep friends. This is a crucial element of social adjustment.

How does your child get along with others? Conflicts with friends are as natural as those that occur between siblings, and even good relationships will have their ups and downs. But persistent complaints that other children don't like her, won't play with her, or pick on her could signal problems with your child's social development. The negative attitudes that develop when your child doesn't get along with her peers frequently spills over from the playground to the classroom. As a result, she may have trouble getting along with teachers and other adults, and problems working cooperatively with other students. These problems make it difficult for your child to focus on schoolwork, and often create disruptions in the classroom. All of these circumstances interfere with learning.

Improving Your Child's Social Skills

Does your child complain often that other kids aren't nice to him? As a parent, you have numerous opportunities to see the way your child gets along with other children. Family gatherings, team sports, church and community activities, and parties offer numerous opportunities for you to watch, unnoticed, your child "in action" with other children. Coaches, scout and club leaders, baby-sitters, and other adults who have regular contact with your child can also offer insights into how he behaves. These individuals can help you validate or dispel any concerns you might have about your child's social skills.

Your child's teacher is in a good position to tell you how your child gets along with other children at school. If there are problems, this could be a difficult conversation. But however painful it is to hear that other kids don't like your child, you can't help her unless you know what the problems are.

The best place to teach social skills to kids is in a social setting. This makes school a good place to start helping a child get along with other children. Most schools have a counselor or psychologist who can help identify your child's areas of difficulty and develop a plan to resolve them.

When talking with your child about his social problems, keep your comments and perspective positive. He doesn't like his inappropriate behaviors any more than you do, but has far less confidence about his ability to change them. Reassure him that you have every confidence that his situation will get better, and that you'll be there for support and guidance. Above all, be patient. It takes time to change behaviors, and it's natural to see some slipping along the way. You and the school might even need to try several different approaches before finding one that works. Social behavior is complex and personal, and what works for one child may not help another.

Back your compassion with firmness.

Some children might benefit from counseling or therapy that takes place outside school and social settings in addition to a school-based intervention. The school counselor or psychologist can guide you in deciding whether to seek additional help for your child, and can provide information about available community resources. Again, it's important to keep in mind your child's school environment so any outside services your child receives are consistent with the school's goals and expectations for her behavior.

Your child needs your support and understanding while she works to change her behaviors and develop new friendships. But back your compassion with firmness – make it clear to your child that however much you understand that this is a difficult time for her, she *must* act in an appropriate and responsible way at school.

■ *Inappropriate Behavior*

When your child violates school rules, fails to follow directions, disrupts the classroom, fights, or steals or destroys property, it's time for swift intervention. Discuss with your child what you've heard from teachers and other school officials about her behavior. Listen carefully, and without interruption, to her side of the story. Occasionally, there are valid extenuating circumstances that explain (though don't excuse) her behavior. Illness, family problems, or a particularly difficult relationship with a classmate may stress your child's behavioral skills to the snapping point. If this appears to be the case, schedule a meeting where you, your child, and your child's teacher can discuss the situation. Regardless of the circumstances, you need to make it clear to your child that you know she has the ability to follow school rules and stay out of trouble, and that's what you expect her to do.

If your child's behavior problems persist, consider setting up the "note" system similar to the one discussed in Chapter 8, *Homework*, page 129. This will give you daily updates on your child's behavior, and reinforce your shared commitment with your child's teacher to bring about change. The teacher may have other ideas about how to help your child improve her behavior. Again, you might need to try several approaches before finding one that works. In most situations, simple plans that directly link behavior and consequences are quite effective. If the problem fails to improve after a reasonable effort, ask the school to evaluate your child for other factors that might be contributing to the situation.

When Your Child Has Conflicts with a Teacher ■

Most children like their teachers. They want to like their teachers, and they want their teachers to like them. The significance of this goes beyond just liking or disliking, however. Your child's relationship with his teacher strongly influences his attitude toward school and learning overall.

As unusual as it is for a child to dislike his teacher, it's fairly common for children to go through brief episodes of complaining that:

- The teacher wasn't fair.

- They got in trouble when whatever happened wasn't their fault.

- The teacher complimented someone else's work, when that person didn't work as hard or do as good a job.

- Their art projects weren't displayed when "everyone" else's were.

Your child's relationship with his teacher influences his attitude toward school and learning.

If you hear these kinds of complaints only occasionally, don't worry about them. After all, teachers are people with personalities and habits, and it's natural for your child to find one or some of them objectionable every now and again. If he complains about his teacher often enough to cause you concern, however, investigate the situation cautiously before approaching the teacher. It isn't always easy to determine if there are other factors creating a problem for your child, or whether he and his teacher truly don't get along.

■ Teaching Styles – and Teachers – Differ

Teaching styles vary widely among teachers. Some teachers are strict, and have high expectations for their students. In such classes, the teacher views herself as the main source of information for her students and responsible for their learning experiences. The teacher structures and directs all classroom activities, and is likely to have numerous classroom rules. Other teachers vest responsibility for learning in their students. In such classes, the teacher views herself as a facilitator to be available when children need her. Even in a classroom environment that may be more noisy and feature fewer rules, the teacher typically has high expectations for student learning.

Your child can be successful in a variety of learning environments. Occasionally, a teacher's approach or style may differ from your child-rearing and educational philosophies. This doesn't mean the teacher is "bad," or that your child won't learn anything in the teacher's class. It simply means that the teacher's view is different from yours. Your child is still likely to have a successful learning experience.

Occasional conflicts are normal and healthy.

Minimize Potential Conflicts ■

While occasional conflicts are not only inevitable but also normal and healthy, there are steps you can take to reduce the likelihood that these conflicts will develop into problems. The first is to understand how teachers approach the process of educating your child.

Teachers enjoy students who want to learn. Children who follow class rules, work cooperatively with other students, and are responsible, persistent, independent, and willing to try hard to master challenging lessons or situations are going to get "breaks" from teachers. This isn't favoritism so much as it is human nature – we all prefer to spend time with people who share our interests and enthusiasms, and teachers are no exception.

The second step is for you to establish a positive relationship with the teacher. This makes it more likely that your child will do the same. These relationships – yours with the teacher and your child's with the teacher – strengthen the collaborative nature of your child's education. You keep an open and regular line of communication that helps you stay on top of what's going on with your child's schoolwork. And you help shape an open and non-threatening environment in which your child is more willing to discuss problems, and so is the teacher.

How to Determine Whether Your Child Might Be Having Problems with a Teacher ■

Complaints are one sign that your child might be having problems with a teacher. There are other signs, however, that are more significant although their connection to school and the teacher might not be as clear.

- There is a sudden change in your child's behavior.

- Your child no longer wants to go to school. He may cry or fuss about going, and may not want to get dressed in the morning.

- Your child's grades drop. She may stop bringing her homework assignments home, and no longer show you her schoolwork.

- Your child has physical symptoms such as stomachaches, or is sick more often than usual.

- Your child tells you, often and loudly, that he hates school.

The presence of these signs doesn't automatically indicate a problem with the teacher. The same signs could point to problems with peers, a bad experience at or after school, or other matters that worry your child.

Ask your child what is bothering her. Keep your questions brief and open, and avoid leading questions that steer her toward a particular response. Try, "You seem unhappy. Is something troubling you?" rather than, "Are you getting along OK with your teacher?" Pay close attention (and even take notes) to what your child views as the cause of her concerns.

If your child does complain about his teacher, write down what he says. Listen, and refrain from making critical comments about the teacher. It's very important for you to stay calm and appear objective. Ask him for specific examples to illustrate his perceptions. Why does he think the problem is the teacher? What does the teacher do that is a problem for him? Let him know that you are concerned and that you will talk to the teacher. When you do, share the results of the discussion with your child.

■ Meeting with the Teacher

When you have concerns, schedule an appointment to meet with the teacher as soon as possible. While you might feel you'd get faster results by talking with the principal, most schools prefer that parents first attempt to resolve problems directly with the teacher. This is often more effective, as well, since it's less threatening and presents your concern in the perspective of cooperation.

Remember, you and the teachers are collaborators in your child's education, not adversaries. It's sometimes easy to lose sight of your shared goal and become angry or defensive, intensifying the problem rather than moving toward a solution. It's important for your child to see that you view the situation as one of partners working together to resolve an issue for your child's benefit.

You See Signs for Concern But Your Child Doesn't Present the Teacher as the Problem

When you see changes in your child's behavior that concern you but your child doesn't complain about her teacher, start by describing your child's behavior before and after the problem surfaced. Ask if the teacher has seen this same pattern. Remember, you still don't know why your child feels the way she does – it may have nothing to do with the teacher. If the cause for the problem is not apparent by the end of this meeting, set up a plan with the teacher to further investigate the matter. Take careful and complete notes to document the meeting.

Your Child Complains Repeatedly About the Teacher

When your child complains repeatedly about her teacher, it's clear that your child sees the teacher as the source of the problem even though there may be other factors at play. Share specific examples of your child's complaints with the teacher. Keep your tone calm and pleasant. This meeting is not a place for anger or accusation; such approaches will only put the teacher (and you) on the defensive and aren't likely to result in any resolution. Listen to the teacher's responses and explanations. Sometimes the problem is one of perspective, and hearing the teacher's comments will lead to resolution. Attempt to close the meeting by agreeing on a plan of action to resolve the problem. Be sure both you and the teacher understand your respective responsibilities.

After the Meeting

Write or type your notes from the meeting, telling what occurred and what you think will happen as a result. Send a copy to the teacher, along with a short letter thanking the teacher for meeting with you. Invite the teacher to give you a call if the teacher disagrees with your representation. Be sure to keep your original notes and a copy of your letter for your records.

Don't wait too long to see changes. For most problems, call the teacher again if your child's behavior is not noticeably different within a week or two. Ask whether the agreed-upon plan has been implemented, and what changes the teacher has noticed. Perhaps the action plan isn't working as expected and needs to be changed. The ideal outcome would be for you and the teacher to agree to a new plan, or to work collaboratively toward uncovering the source of your child's unhappiness. If the phone call leaves you feeling that nothing is likely to change, it's time to get the principal involved.

Don't wait too long to see changes.

When to Meet with the Principal ■

We mentioned earlier that schools prefer that parents attempt to work out problems with the teacher before drawing in the principal. However, there are a few circumstances in which the problem appears serious enough to circumvent the usual procedure. Examples would be a teacher who calls children names (such as stupid) or belittles them in front of others, tears up student papers in anger, engages in physical abuse or inappropriate physical contact, and other behaviors that seem considerably removed from what you expect. Principals usually act quickly to resolve such concerns.

It's also time to involve the principal if you've met with the teacher on several occasions and you still see no changes in your child's situation or behavior, or if you believe the teacher has failed to implement the agreed-upon plan. If this happens, call the principal and explain your concerns. Fax, mail, or hand-carry copies of your notes and any other documentation to the principal. This gives the principal more objective information with which to evaluate the situation and make a decision about appropriate intervention.

The principal may ask to meet with you, alone or with the teacher. Bring copies of previous documentation with you to the meeting. This helps keep the meeting focused on the facts, which will help you move toward resolution. Again, it's important to take thorough and detailed notes, and to send copies to the principal and the teacher after the meeting is over.

■ *When to Take Your Concerns Further*

Most conflicts with teachers end after a meeting or two that involves the principal. In rare situations, you may need to contact a representative at the school district level. This might be an assistant superintendent or other administrative official. Documentation is particularly important when you bring a concern to this level.

What to Tell Your Child ■

You want your child to believe that the teacher and the school will work with you to resolve the problem. Your child will be in school for quite a few years, and you want her perceptions to be as positive as possible.

Let your child know what progress you're making toward resolving the problem. Don't belittle the teacher or run down the school. Though you may be angry or frustrated with the situation, such negative comments strongly affect your child's attitude toward school and the teacher. He is already upset and unhappy, and you don't want to make things worse. Your calm and professional, yet concerned, manner sets a powerful example for him about how to effectively resolve problems.

Resolving Student/Teacher Problems Successfully ■

The better your relationship with your child's school and teacher, the higher the probability that you'll be able to resolve problems quickly. Parents who are most successful in generating changes for their children are those who:

- Approach the teacher in a calm, non-threatening, collaborative manner. "Susan is having some problems, and I'd like to work together to resolve them."

You want your child's perceptions to be as positive as possible.

- Present specific details and examples – "before this year, Jesse got all A's and now he's getting C's" – rather than vague accusations – "I don't think Jordan is being challenged enough."

- Show willingness to try the teacher's or school's recommendations for solving the problem.

- Keep detailed and accurate documentation of all meetings that occur during the process of trying to resolve a problem.

Remember:

1) Most teachers are as concerned about your child's educational experiences as you are, and want to resolve any problems that interfere with your child's learning.

2) When your child is having problems, you'll need to get involved. Be prepared to invest additional time.

CHAPTER CONCEPTS

- Distinguish a minor from a major problem.

- Recognize warning signs for academic problems.

- Recognize warning signs for social/behavioral problems.

- Learn whether your child can't or won't do the work.

- Work with teachers to find solutions for your child's problems.

- Find additional assistance for your child's academic problems.

- Improve social skills.

- Deal with your child's inappropriate behavior in school.

- Resolve conflicts between your child and the teacher.

BENEFITS & RESULTS

You prevent minor problems from becoming major.

You work with the teacher as allies
to resolve your child's problems.

You change *won't-do* kids to *will-do* students.

Your child gets the additional help he needs to be successful.

You resolve your child's conflict with the teacher
in ways most beneficial to your child.

CHAPTER 12

Finding More Time

*Wouldn't it be great to add
just five minutes to each hour?*

You'd gain two hours a day! Problem
is, you still wouldn't have enough time
to do all you need to do. No matter how
you try to stretch the day, it always
seems a few hours short. So where —
and how — do you find more time?

Delegation works at the office – it can work at home, too.

■ Share Household Chores

As the parent, you no doubt carry the biggest burden of household chores. Some of this load just comes with the territory. After all, you're responsible for assuring that your household runs smoothly and meets your family's needs. That doesn't mean you can't delegate – if it works at the office, it can work at home.

Getting other family members to accept their fair share is easiest when you start young. Even preschoolers can help out with basic tasks like setting the table and putting their clean clothes away. Older children can handle additional responsibilities, from taking out the trash to doing the dishes. All children can keep their bedrooms picked up and put their dirty laundry in the hamper. No, we haven't parted ways with reality — we said *can*, not do! (See Chapter 6, *Building "Little Engines Who Can,"* for tips on how to make this happen.)

■ Meals

Forget Old Mother Hubbard. Today's busy parent needs well-stocked cupboards (not to mention refrigerator and freezer). For economy of time and budget, buy in bulk whenever possible. You'll spend less time shopping, and always have something on hand when plans go astray. Put your kids to work clipping coupons for items your household purchases. And unless the savings are worth the additional gas and time it takes to drive around, do most of your shopping at one store. Rather than shop around, check around. Many stores honor competitors' coupons, making comparison shopping unnecessary.

Store breakfast items in lower cupboards where your kids can reach them. Most kids enjoy being able to choose and fix what they want for breakfast. Does your child prefer cold pizza or leftover chicken to cereal and toast? Such items are just as nutritious, and less hassle for you (as long as you haven't planned to revive them for dinner). Keep nutritious snacks in easy-to-reach places, too, to handle after-school hunger attacks.

Older children often enjoy having responsibility for one meal a week that they plan and prepare (with your help as needed). This takes you off the hot seat for the most difficult question of the day, "What's for dinner?" and puts an end to complaining about your choices. You're not completely free, of course — most children need help or at least guidance in the kitchen, so you'll have to be close by (maybe sitting at the table enjoying a newspaper untouched by other hands). All school-age children can at least help set and clear the table.

Older children enjoy having responsibility for planning and preparing one meal a week

When it's your turn to cook, choose meals that are quick, nutritious, and need little preparation. Double recipes to fix extra portions that you can freeze to serve another time. Use a crockpot or slow oven to let meals cook while you're at work, and your dinner can practically serve itself (this works well when not all family members can eat together, too). Many appliances have timers that will automatically turn the device on, run it at the temperature and for the time you set, and turn it off. Early dinner times often work better than late. Most kids are "starving" when they come home from school, and everyone is tired.

While you can't buy time, you can buy convenience. Order a meal delivered once a week or so. Many restaurants offer phone-ahead carryout service, and many grocery stores feature complete takeout meals you can pick up on your way home. And of course, there's always delivery pizza!

Laundry ■

Without a doubt, one of the most appealing features of futuristic fiction is the absence of laundry. Whether technology has come up with fabrics that never get dirty or clothes somehow clean themselves, space-age parents seem relieved of what is a never-ending chore in this age! You can't make laundry go away, of course. But you can make it easier.

- Choose low-care fabrics that require no special cleaning or ironing.

- Make each family member accountable for personal laundry. If it's not in the hamper, it doesn't get washed. (Don't panic — no child yet has suffered brain damage from wearing dirty socks to school.)

- Wash just once a week.

Teach older children how to sort laundry, fill and run the washer, and run the dryer. Beware the learning curve, however. What you know about laundry, you've learned over a lifetime of trial and error (everyone has once-elegant clothing that's now barely suitable for dressing dolls or a full complement of pink sports socks). For minimum anguish, separate fine washables from the regular laundry, and do these yourself.

> *Flex-time allows you to structure your hours around your children's schedules.*

■ Work

Some people find telecommuting gives them the best of all worlds. There's no commute, office hours start when you get there, and office politics are between you and your cat. As traffic congestion becomes a significant problem in many urban areas, most jobs at least offer flex-time. This allows you to choose when you'd like to come in and when you'd like to leave (usually within a certain range). Some employers let you balance your work hours over a week or a pay period; others want to see your smiling face for a certain number of hours each day. A standard work week might be five 8-hour days, four 10-hour days, or even three 12-hour days.

Two-parent families often structure their work schedules to have one parent home in the morning and one home in the afternoon, so someone is always with the kids. With younger children, this might even mean working different shifts. As your children grow older, their days fill with additional activities, from study groups to athletic teams, that make this schedule-sharing less drastic. Do short errands during your breaks and lunch times. Choose direct deposit for your paycheck, and take "go to the bank" off your list.

The real key to finding more time rests not just with looking for time you're not presently using, but also in looking at how you spend your time. Do you feel there's just nothing you can cut from your life? Here's a quick check. Grab a piece of paper and a pencil (or pen or even crayon, whatever is handy). Draw a line down the center of the paper. Label one side "Must Do." Label the other side "What Will Happen If I Don't." Mentally go through your day. Write everything you think you have to do in the column labeled "Must Do." In the other column, write what will happen if you don't do it. Obviously, there are activities and tasks you just can't do without. But how much of what you think you have to do could you actually drop from your life without adverse consequence? Try dropping a few for a week or so — see if it helps you find more time.

■ *Appointments and Errands*

Schedule appointments together for your kids — doctor, dentist, optometrist. You can even toss yours into the lineup for maximum efficiency. Batch your errands, too. Drop off dry-cleaning on your way to or from work. Take your prescriptions to the pharmacy before you do other shopping, and pick up your medications when you're finished. Do your favorite stores offer mail-order service? Take advantage of this time-saver — and save money, too, distanced from those in-store "specials" that offer prices too good to be true for items you didn't know you needed.

■ *Banking*

Does your bank offer telebanking or online banking? These services let you conduct your banking business at your convenience, without waiting in line or even leaving your home (or office). If you have direct deposit for your paycheck and direct pay for bills where this is an option, you might never see the inside of a bank again! Establish and maintain a good home filing system to keep all of your finances in order.

Transportation ■

Is public transportation available between where you live and where you work? If so, give it a try. You gain 20 to 30 minutes (or more) with someone else worrying about traffic — perfect for catching up on your recreational reading, the work you didn't quite finish yesterday, or even sleep. If public transportation is not an option, consider carpooling for the same advantages (except when it's your turn to drive). Have you become your child's personal chauffeur? Rotate driving responsibility with other parents, or combine trips to the mall with errands you already have to run. If you drive your kids to and from school each day, consider forming a carpool with other parents in your neighborhood.

■ *Time for You*

When was the last time you read a novel from the "New Books" section? Listened to music you enjoy? Soaked in the tub without a child pounding on the bathroom door? Watched a ballgame on television with no cartoon interruptions? Family and work could each easily consume every waking moment, and you're balancing both! As you reclaim more time from your day, set some of it aside just for you. Small investments yield amazingly large returns when it comes to these "me-minutes."

■ *Make Finding Time a Family Activity*

You can't add time to your day. But you can structure your day to get the most from the hours (and minutes) it contains. Involve all family members in finding ways to spend more time together. Not only will this benefit your child's learning and school experiences, but odds are, you all will find new activities to enjoy.

CHAPTER CONCEPTS

- Ways to cut time spent on household chores.

- Tips to make meals less time-consuming.

- Making meals a family together time.

- Tips on simplifying your busy life.

- Spending less time on appointments and errands.

BENEFITS & RESULTS

Have more time with your family.

Find time just for you.

Accomplish a family goal by working together.

Educational Games

GEOGRAPHY	MATH	SCIENCE	STRATEGIES
LANGUAGE	RECOGNITION	SPELLING	VOCABULARY

NAME OF GAME	MANUFACTURER	AGES	SUBJECT CATEGORY
20 Questions / People, Places & Things	Natural Wonders	7-12	★ ♞
20 Questions / Nature & Science	Natural Wonders	7-12	⚛ ♞
24 Game Primer	Suntex International Inc.	5-Up	✚ Basic facts
24 Game Primer Algebra	Suntex International Inc.	13-Up	✚
24 Game Primer Exponents	Suntex International Inc.	11-Up	✚
24 Game Primer Decimals	Suntex International Inc.	11-Up	✚
Alphabet Soup	Parker Preschool	3-6	╱
Animal Families (memory game)	Milton Bradley	3-6	★ 📖
Axies and Allies	Milton Bradley	12-Up	★ Thinking skills / economics
Balderdash	Games Gang, Ltd.	10-Up	📖
Bank Account	Creative Teaching Insights	Grade 5-12	✚
Bertie's Bottle Caps (color matching)	Golden	3-6	★ 📖
Bingo Beginner	Pressman	4-6	📖 Letter recognition
Blurt!	Webster	10 -Up	📖
Boggle Jr. Numbers	Parker Brothers	Preschool	✚
Boggle Master	Parker Brothers	8-Up	╱
Brain Quest	University Games	Grade1-6	All subjects
Brick by Brick Puzzles	Binary Arts Comp.	All ages	Problem-solving

GEOGRAPHY	MATH	SCIENCE	STRATEGIES
✎ LANGUAGE	★ RECOGNITION	🄰🄱🄲 SPELLING	◣ VOCABULARY

NAME OF GAME	MANUFACTURER	AGES	SUBJECT CATEGORY
Clue, Clue Jr.	Parker Brothers	8-Up	★ ♞
CNN-The Game	Game Plan	12-Up	🌐 ★
Connect Four (vertical checkers)	Milton Bradley	8-Up	Visual problem-solving
Crack the Case	Milton Bradley	9-Up	★ Logical thinking
Creature Factory (visual discrimination)	Educational Insights	3-6	★
Cribbage	Pressman	8-Up	✚
Deluxe Skip Bo	Mattel	7-Up	# Recognition / Problem-solving
Dino Math Tracks	Learning Resources	6-Up	✚ Problem-solving / Place value counting
Dinosaur Domino	Creative Toys, Ltd.	6-12	Word recognition
Dominoes	Pavillion	6-Up	✚
Don't Wake Daddy (color matching)	Parker Brothers	4-Up	✎
Enchanted Forest	Ravensburger	6-Up	♞ Strategies
Erector Sets		8-Up	♞ Problem-solving
Game of Life	Milton Bradley	9-Up	✚ ★
Gestures	Milton Bradley	12-Up	★ ◣
Giant Dice	Child's Play Int, Ltd.	6-12	✚
Go To The Head of the Class	Milton Bradley	8-Up	★ General knowledge
Hangman	Milton Bradley	8-Up	★ ◣
Hi Ho Cheery-O (counting)	Golden	3-6	✚
Human Body Bingo	Safari, Ltd.	8-Up	★ ⚛
Husker Du?	The Games Gang Ltd.	5-Up	Memory game
Into the Forest	Ampersand Press	7-Up	⚛
IQ Games	Educational Insights	8-Up	★ ◣

🌐 GEOGRAPHY	✚ MATH	⚛ SCIENCE	♞ STRATEGIES
╱ LANGUAGE	★ RECOGNITION	🄰🄱🄲 SPELLING	📕 VOCABULARY

NAME OF GAME	MANUFACTURER	AGES	SUBJECT CATEGORY
IQ Games U.S. History	Educational Insights	8-Up	★
IQ Game Wonders	Educational Insights	8-Up	★ ⚛
Jeopardy	Tyco	Teen-Up	★ 📕
Letter Perfect (word games)	Educational Insights	4-Up	╱ ★ 📕
Lucy Cousins' Maisy Game	Briarpatch Inc.	3-6	★ Matching
Make 7	Pressman	7-Up	✚ ♞
Match & Spell	Ravensburger	5-8	🄰🄱🄲
Math Race	Ravensburger	6-10	✚
Math Games	Educational Insight	Primary	✚ ★
Math Games	Educational Insight	Intermediate	✚ ★
Math Magic	Ravensburger	5-7	✚
Monopoly	Parker Brothers	8-Up	✚ ★ ♞
Monopoly Jr.	Parker Brothers	5-8	✚ ★ ♞
Name That Word	Creative Teaching Associate	5-12	★ 📕
Number Rings	Orota Industries Ltd.	8-12	✚
Opposites	Ravensburger	3-Up	📕
Original Rummikub	Pressman	8-Up	✚
Othello	Pressman	8-Up	Generic problem-solving
Outburst	Golden/Hersch	Teen-Up	📕
Payday	Parker Brothers	8-Up	╱ ✚
Pictionary	Milton Bradley	12-Up	╱ 📕
Pictionary Jr.	Milton Bradley	8-14	╱ 📕
Presto Chang-O	Educational Insights	5-Up	✚
Princess (a cooperative game)	Family Pastimes	4-7	★
Puzzles		All Ages	♞ Problem-solving
Rummikub	Pressman	5-Up	# Sequence

GEOGRAPHY	MATH	SCIENCE	STRATEGIES	
LANGUAGE	RECOGNITION	SPELLING	VOCABULARY	

NAME OF GAME	MANUFACTURER	AGES	SUBJECT CATEGORY
Rummikub 500	Pressman	8-Up	[Math] [Strategies] Problem-solving
Scrabble	Milton Bradley	8-Up	[Language] [Recognition] [Spelling]
Six Cubes	Fun & Games Group	10-Up	[Math]
Spellway	Pressman	6-Up	[Spelling] [Vocabulary]
Super Clerk	Creative Teaching Insights	Grade 3-8	[Math] [Recognition]
Take Off!	Take Off, Inc.	8-Up	[Geography] [Recognition]
The Allowance Game	Lakeshore Curriculum	7-10	[Math] [Recognition] [Strategies]
Traverse (chess & checkers combined)	Educational Insights	7-Up	[Strategies] Problem-solving
Triple Yahtzee	Milton Bradley	8-Up	[Math]
Trivia Adventure for Kids		Grades 2-8	All subjects
True Science	Aristoplay	10-Up	[Recognition] [Science]
Ungame	Talicor	5-Up	Cooperative learning / communication
Uno	Mattel	7-Up	[Math]
Upwords (a 3D word game)	Milton Bradley	10-Up	[Math]
Where Do I Belong? (Animals)	Creative Toys, LTD.	Preschool	[Science]
Where Have All The Salmon Gone	Ness Adventures, Inc.	8-Up	[Recognition] [Science]
Where in the USA is Carmen Sandiego?	University Games	8-Up	[Geography] [Recognition] [Strategies]
Where in the World is Carmen Sandiego?	University Games	10-Up	[Geography] [Recognition] [Strategies]
Word Yahtzee	Milton Bradley	8-Up	[Language] [Math]
Yahtzee	Milton Bradley	8-Up	[Math]

Good Websites for Kids

There are hundreds, maybe thousands, of websites on the Internet that have something to do with kids.

The problem with trying to list them is that they tend to come and go. It's the nature of the Internet (and indeed one of the attributes that makes it so popular) for information to change frequently.

A handful of sites are set up as clearinghouses – they locate and link to other sites that feature relevant content. These sites generally monitor the links they list to make sure they remain active. In this appendix, we've listed some that offer good content for children, including help with school assignments and homework. Remember, while we've researched these sites for this book, we can't guarantee that by the time you visit, they'll still be operational.

■ A Word of Caution

Most major websites for kids go to great lengths to assure that the content they carry or link to is reasonably safe for children. Most web browsers offer blocking controls to help parents regulate how far and to where their youthful cyberadventurers may travel, and numerous vendors sell software featuring more stringent filters and controls to accomplish the same objective. The Internet is a vast repository of information, however, and no safeguards are foolproof. We urge you to talk with your child about "safe surfing," and to monitor your child's Internet activities. And be advised: nearly all sites include commercial advertising.

■ Special Note

Sites with lots of whiz-bang special effects may require you to download special plug-ins that allow animated graphics and sounds to function on your computer. Most plug-ins are free via download (excluding any telephone or online service provider charges) and easy to load.

Kid-Focused Websites ■

http://www.yahoo.com/Society_and_Culture/
Cultures_and_Groups/Children/
Links_for_Kids/

If this lengthy e-address overwhelms you, you can reach it by entering "kids" as your search query on the Yahoo search site (**http://www.yahoo.com**). Lists thousands of sites for kids, from entertainment to research. Organized by subject category.

http://www.dig.com/

Disney Internet Guide. Convenient listings of a wide variety of subjects arranged by category. While DIG controls the content at its site, it cannot do so once your child links to an external site - we recommend parental supervision. ABC News site, for example, allows access to any and all news reports. Homework helper links guide children to a wide range of resource materials, from the online version of Encyclopedia Britannica (limited access unless you subscribe) to categories as diverse as sports and neuroscience.

http://www.yahooligans.com/

Yahooligans. Website for kids sponsored by the popular search site Yahoo.com. Lots of fun stuff and homework help, too. "Ask an Expert" lets kids direct their questions to experts from Mr. Science to the Grammar Lady. However, site also links to "Ask Orkin," the homepage for the national pest control company (which, to its credit, does offer some, um, interesting information about cockroaches and other creepy critters).

http://tristate.pgh.net/~pinch13/

B.J. Pinchbeck's Homework Helper. Developed by Pennsylvania 11 year-old Bruce Pinchbeck, Jr. and his father. "If you can't find it here, then you just can't find it," says the welcome banner. Site has received more than 100 web awards and lists more than 500 websites to help kids find any information that they need. Appears to receive regular updating; many references and resources.

http://www.startribune.com/stonline/html/ special/homework/

Homework Help. Produced by the Minneapolis/St. Paul Star Tribune. Many useful links and resources, conveniently organized by category. While one category is Elementary School Topics, navigation in this area might require assistance from an adult. Kids can direct questions to teachers.

http://www.nickelodeon.com/

Site features favorite Nick cartoon characters and of course, unabashed promotion of Nick movies and other events. Mostly entertainment, with Nick Jr. offering activities and games specially for preschoolers. Despite the useful sound of its name, the section called "The Big Help" promotes Nickelodeon's campaign to get kids involved in community improvement projects rather than offering any sort of homework or other assistance.

http://ykd.headbone.com/

Headbone Zone. Mostly commercial, some educational resources. Linked from many local newspapers.

http://www.disney.com/

Disney. As commercial as you might expect. Lots of entertainment, with special areas for families as well as stuff just for kids.

http://www.nypl.org/branch/kids/onlion.html

"On-Lion" for Kids is a site developed by the New York Public Library. It has many sections from which to choose, from fact to fiction, for ages preschool through middle grades. Among other things, it contains a wealth of information on books, booklists, authors, characters. Activities and information abound!

http://www.ala.org/parentspage/greatsites/amazing.html

This site developed by the American Library Association describes and recommends over 700 sites for children, preschool through 14 years, on all subjects from the arts and literature to science and technology. Sites for booklists are to be found here as are sites to which children can contribute their own writing. Great ideas for parents and kids!

http://www.parentsplace.com

This commercial site has many, many suggestions and ideas for parents to use with children in areas from science to literature. Click into the Reading Room and find a listing of hundreds of book reviews. This site also contains a section on science and nature activities and many more parenting topics.

Recommended Reading

1. **What's a Time-Starved Parent to Do**

   Peel, Kathy (1997) *The Family Manager's Guide for Working Moms*. New York: Penguin.

   Pillsbury, G. Linda (1994) *Survival Tips for Working Moms*. Los Angeles: Perspective Publishing.

2. **Ready to Learn**

   Glove, B. and Shepard, J. (1989) *The Family Fitness Handbook*. New York: Penguin.

   Jacobson, M.F. and Maxwell, B. (1994) *What Are We Feeding Our Kids*. New York: Workman Publishing.

   Kamen, B. and Kamen, S. (1983) *Kids Are What They Eat*. New York: Arco Publishing.

   Kleinman, R.E. and Jellinek, M.S. (1994) *Let Them Eat Cake*. New York: Villard Books.

   Kuntzleman, C. (1988) *Healthy Kids for Life*. New York: Pocket Books.

   Schauss, A., Freidlander, M. and Meyer, A. (1991) *Eating for A's*. New York: Pocket Books.

   Smith, L. (1996) *How to Raise a Healthy Child*. New York: M. Evans & Co.

3. *Building Positive Attitudes Toward School*

Baron, B., Baron, C., and MacDonald, B. (1983) *What Did You Learn in School Today?* New York: Warner Books.

Calkins, L. (1997) *Raising Lifelong Learners.* Reading, MA: Addison-Wesley.

Dargatz, J. (1993) *52 Ways to Help Your Child Do Better in School.* Nashville: Thomas Nelson Publishers.

Hemstetter, S. (1989) *Predictive Parenting: What To Say When You Talk To Your Kids.* New York: Pocket Books.

Schaefer, C.E. and DiGeronimo, T.F. (1991) *How to Help Your Child Get the Most Out of School.* New York: Plume.

4. *Furnishing Your Home for Learning*

Appendix – Listing of 90 age-appropriate educational games

DeFrancis, B. (1994) *The Parents' Resource Almanac.* Holbrook, MA: Bob Adams, Inc.

Donavin, D.P. ed. (1992) *American Library Association Best of the Best for Children: Books, Software, Magazines, Videos, Audio, Toys, Travel.* Chicago: ALA.

Einstein, D. (1996) *PCs For Busy People.* New York: Osborne.

Keiser, G. (1996) *The Family PC Guide to Homework.* New York: Hyperion.

Kraynak, K. (1996) *The Complete Idiot's Guide to PCs* (4th edition). Indianapolis: QUE.

Miramker, C. and Elliot, A. (1996) *Great Software for Kids & Parent.* Chicago: IDG Books.

Oppenheim, J. and Oppenheim, S. (1995) *The Best Toys, Books, and Videos for Kids.* New York: Harper Collins.

Pouge, D. (1996) *MACS for DUMMIES* (4th edition) Chicago: IDG Books.

Werdel, Hilary (1998) *Discover Educational Toys for Children* (2nd edition). San Francisco: Scholar Books.

5. *Opportunities to Learn: Making the Best Use of Available Time*

Dargatz, Z. (1993) *52 Ways to Help Your Child Do Better in School.* Nashville: Thomas Nelson Publishers.

DeFrancis, B. (1994) *The Parents' Resource Almanac.* Holbrook, MA: Bob Adams, Inc.

Rimm, Sylvia B. (1996) *Dr. Sylvia Rimm's Smart Parenting: How to Parent So Children Will Learn.* New York: Three Rivers Press.

Trelease, J. (1995) *The Read Aloud Handbook.* New York: Penguin.

6. *Building "Little Engines Who Can"*

Cogan, V. (1992) *Boosting the Underachiever.* New York: Berkley Books

Cutright, M. (1994) *Growing up Confident.* New York: Doubleday.

Davidson, A. and Davidson, R. (1996) *How Good Parents Raise Great Kids.* New York: Warner Books.

Dinkmeyer, D. and McKay, G.D. (1982) *Raising a Responsible Child.* New York: Simon and Schuster.

Faber, A. and Mazlish, E. (1982) *How To Talk So Kids Will Listen & Listen So Kids Will Talk.* New York: Avon Books.

Glenn, S.H. and Nelsen, J. (1989) *Raising Self-Reliant Children in a Self-Indulgent World.* Rocklin, CA: Prima Publishing.

Helmstetter, S. (1989) *Predictive Parenting: What To Say When You Talk To Your Kids.* New York: Pocket Books.

Isaacs, S. and Ritchey, W. (1989) *"I Think I Can, I Know I Can!"* New York: St. Martin's Press.

Marston, S. (1990) *The Magic of Encouragement.* New York: Pocket Books.

Rich, D. (1992) *Mega Skills.* New York: Houghton Mifflin.

Rimm, Sylvia B. (1996) *Dr. Sylvia Rimm's Smart Parenting: How to Parent So Children Will Learn.* New York: Three Rivers Press.

Rosemond, J. (1989) *John Rosemond's Six Point Plan.* Kansas City, MO: Andrews and McNeil.

Rosemond, J. (1990) *Parent Power.* Kansas City, MO: Andrews and McNeil.

7. *Developing a Partnership with Your Child's School*

Baron, B., Baron, C. and MacDonald, B. (1983) *What Did You Learn in School Today?* New York: Warner Books.

Bean, R. (1991) *How To Help Your Children Succeed In School.* Los Angeles: Price, Stern Sloan, Inc.

Greene, L.J. (1991) *1001 Ways to Improve Your Child's Schoolwork.* New York: Dell

Harrington, D. and Young, L. (1993) *School Savvy.* New York: Farrar, Straus, and Giroux.

Schaefer, C.E. and DiGeronimo, T.F. (1991) *How to Help Your Child Get the Most Out of School.* New York: Plume.

8. *Homework*

Nemko, M. (1989) *How to Get a Private School Education in a Public School*. Berkely, CA: Ten Speed Press.

Rosemond, J. (1990) *Ending the Homework Hassle*. New York: Andrew McMeel.

Schaefer, C.E. and DiGeronimo, T.F. (1991) *How to Help Your Child Get the Most Out of School*. New York: Plume.

Sonna, L.A. (1990) *The Homework Solution*. Charlotte, VT: Williamson Publishing Company.

9. *So You Want to Help Your Child with Schoolwork*

Baron, B., Baron, C., and MacDonald, B. (1983) *What Did You Learn in School Today?* New York: Warner Books.

Calkins, L. (1997) *Raising Lifelong Learners*. Reading, MA: Addison-Wesley.

Edwards, S.A. and Maloy, R.W. (1992) *Kids Have All the Write Stuff*. New York: Penguin.

Ledson, S. (1987) *Raising Brighter Children*. New York: Walker and Company.

Rein, R.P. and Rein, R. (1994) *How to Develop Your Child's Gifts and Talents During the Elementary Years*. Los Angeles: Lowell House.

Schaefer, C.E. and DiGeronimo, T.F. (1991) *How to Help Your Child Get the Most Out of School*. New York: Plume.

Shermer, M. (1995) *Teach Your Child Science*. Los Angeles: Lowell House.

Shure, M. and DiGeronimo, T.F. (1994) *Raising a Thinking Child*. New York: Henry Holt & Co.

Yablun, R. (1995) *How to Develop Your Child's Gifts in Math*. Los Angeles: Lowell House.

---

10. *Learning and Television*

Bennett, R. and Bennett. (1994) *Kick the TV Habit*. New York: Penguin.

Chen, M. (1994) *The Smart Parent's Guide to Kids' TV*. San Francisco, CA: KQED Books.

Healy, J.M. (1990) *Endangered Minds*. New York: Simon and Schuster.

Singer, D.G., Singer, J.L. and Zuckerman, D.M. (1990) *Use TV to Your Child's Advantage*. Reston, VA: Acropolis Books Ltd.

Winn, M. (1985) *The Plug-In Drug*. New York: Penguin Books.

11. *When Your Child Has Problems*

Anderson, W., Chitwood, S., and Hayden, D. (1997) *Negotiating the Special Education Maze*. Bethesda, MD: Woodbine House.

Garber, S.I., Garber, M.D., and Spinoza, R.F. (1996) *Beyond Ritalin*. New York: Harper Perennial

Greene, L.J. (1991) *1001 Ways to Improve Your Child's Schoolwork*. New York: Dell.

Ingersoll, B. (1988) *Your Hyperactive Child*. New York: Doubleday.

Schaefer, C.E. and DiGeronimo, T.F. (1991) *How to Help Your Child Get the Most Out of School*. New York: Plume.

12. *Finding More Time*

Hedrick, L.H. (1994) *365 Ways to Save Time with Kids*. New York: Hearst Books.

Pillsbury, L.G. (1994) *Survival Tips for Working Moms*. Los Angeles: Perspective Publishing.

INDEX

About the Authors

■ *John E. Beaulieu, Ph.D.* received his M.A. in Special Education from the University of Colorado and his Ph.D. in Educational Psychology from the University of Oregon. He has worked in the field of education for over 20 years. He has been both a regular and special education teacher. He has also done work in school psychology. John spent 10 years at Pacific Lutheran University as a professor teaching pre-service teachers. He is currently President/CEO of Peer Tutor Press, a company which creates educational materials to help children and adults tutor other students. John lives with his wife Ann and his daughter Emily. Living with two working parents, Emily graduated valedictorian of her class. She is currently a junior majoring in International Studies in the honors college at the University of Washington in Seattle, Washington.

■ *Alex Granzin, Ph.D.* was born and raised in New Orleans, Louisiana where he attended the University of New Orleans and graduated with a B.A. degree in mathematics in 1967. In 1975 he received a Ph.D. from the University of Oregon in curriculum and instruction. He has served as a consultant to a variety of school districts, conducted social science research, taught graduate and undergraduate classes at the University of Oregon, and served as a school psychologist in Springfield, Oregon for the past eighteen years. He is married and has a fourteen year old daughter who recently graduated from middle school with honors.

■ *Deborah S. Romaine* has published several books and more than 300 articles. She has an M.A. in English/Creative Writing from the University of Washington. The mother of two school-age children, she works full-time as a writer.

SEND FOR YOUR FREE COPY!

ARE WE ALMOST THERE?

ALL KINDS OF GAMES FOR ANY ROAD TRIP

...a collection of 33 educational car games for your children.

Available only through the mail with the coupon below.

(No phone requests please.)

Fill out coupon and enclose four 32-cent stamps or $1.00 for postage.